Planet Surf

For
My Lovely Marisa

Planet Surf

RYAN A. SMITH

HISTORY & CULTURE / 50 GREATEST DESTINATIONS

THUNDER BAY
P·R·E·S·S
San Diego, California

Thunder Bay Press
An imprint of the Baker & Taylor Publishing Group, 10350 Barnes Canyon Road, San Diego, CA 92121
www.thunderbaybooks.com

All notations of errors or omissions should be addressed to Thunder Bay Press, Editorial Department, at the above address. All other correspondence (author inquiries, permissions) concerning the content of this book should be addressed to Elephant Book Company Limited, 35 Fournier Street, London E1 6QE, United Kingdom
Email: info@elephantbookcompany.com

Editorial Director: Will Steeds
Project Editor: Laura Ward
Cover and Interior Design: Louise Turpin
Picture research: Ryan A. Smith
Cartographer: Eugene Fleury
Production: Robert Paulley
Color reproduction: Modern Age Repro House Ltd, Hong Kong

Thunder Bay Press Editor: Bonnie Vandewater

ISBN-13: 978-1-59223-985-6
ISBN-10: 1-59223-985-4

Library of Congress Cataloging-in-Publication Data available upon request.

Printed in China

1 2 3 4 5 6 7 13 12 11 10 09

Contents

Foreword

The fascination with breaking waves goes back as far as biblical times, but it was in the late eighteenth and early nineteenth centuries that traveling men laid down the roots of surf stoke. In December 1777, as Captain James Cook was strolling on the beach at Point Venus on the island of Tahiti, Cook remarked of a native man riding waves in his canoe, seemingly just for kicks: "*I could not help concluding that this man felt the most supreme pleasure while he was driven on so fast and so smoothly by the sea . . .*"

Exactly right, Cap'n. And it didn't stop there. In the early nineteenth century, the roguish English aristocrat and poet George Gordon Noel Byron—Lord Byron—had ocean adventures of his own while traveling from the Atlantic to the Adriatic and the Black Sea. Byron rhapsodized about waves, and riding them, in his poem *Childe Harold's Pilgrimage:*

And I have loved them, Ocean! and my joy
Of youthful sports was on thy breast to be Borne,
like shy bubbles, onward;
from a boy I wanton'd with thy breakers . . .
And laid my hand upon thy mane—as I do here.

A few decades later, Richard Henry Dana Jr., another young, educated seafarer, was playing out Byronic fantasies of his own along the coast of California, where he landed on the beach at Santa Barbara in January 1835. As he recorded: ". . . the great seas were rolling in, in regular lines, growing larger and larger as they approached the shore and hanging over the beach upon which they were to break, when their tops would curl over and turn white with foam, and, beginning at one extreme of the line, break rapidly to the other, as a long card-house falls when the children knock down the cards at one end."

Here in the twenty-first century, the obsession with point breaks, reef breaks, outer reefs, beach breaks, sandbars, jetties, pier breaks, bomboras, tidal bores, ship wakes and all waves, natural and man-made, are at the foundation of a surf industry that is worth billions of dollars and provides livelihoods for tens of thousands of people.

The perfect wave is the result of disparate events having occurred over centuries or millenia. Waves break through reefs and along points and over sandbars that were shaped, seemingly, by happy accident, even if the same variables that are at the heart of chaos theory may indeed have coincided to produce such fortunate results. The volcano that deposited the perfectly formed lava reef; the creek that rolled down the many tons of cobblestones; the freshwater river that eroded the hole in the coral reef—all of this happened by chance. There are millions of reefs, rivermouths, points, and headlands around the world, but those that are ideally situated to turn rolling swells into perfect waves may be counted in their dozens.

Over the horizon, hundreds or maybe thousands of miles away, storms of unimaginable force expend their winds over just the right amount of fetch, pointed in just the right direction, to unleash a train of waves which form up in ranks like perfect soldiers, then organize their power and majestic length as they roll across thousands of miles of open ocean.

When a swell that has traveled for many days meets a point or a reef that has been formed over the millenia—and the local variables of tide and wind are in alignment—the result is a perfect wave, bubbling wantonly, and bringing a supreme pleasure to those willing to brave the secrets of the sea.

—Ben Marcus

The Story

# of Surfing

The first surfers

No one knows definitively when, where, or how surfing began. Some anthropologists believe that the first people to ride waves on one-person water craft may have been West African or Peruvian. Anthropologists report that Pre-Inca fishermen were carried back to shore on *caballitos*–pea-pod-shaped boats made of bundled totora reeds–by the power of breaking swells as early as 3000 BC. Others point to the southeastern Pacific Ocean, particularly the Society and Marquesas islands of Polynesia, as the birthplace of surfing. But what historians do agree on is the fact that stand-up surfing, as we know it, began in Hawaii around 1000 AD and was refined there, unnoticed by the rest of the world, for hundreds of years.

Surfing in "precontact Hawaii," generally defined as the time period before Captain James Cook arrived at the islands in the late eighteenth century, was not only recreational but also held religious, cultural, and hierarchical significance. Men, women, and children of all ages played in the surf, and entire villages sometimes escaped to the beach to enjoy the waves. Hawaiians held surfing challenges and gambled everything from food and livestock to servitude and romance, even wagering the life of the loser. Special gods were often given offerings, ceremonies, and chants in rituals asking them to bless the islands with good surf. The creation of surfboards was a careful and important practice that was surrounded by tradition and taboo. Surfing was also performed as a

Below Naked Sandwich Islanders enjoy an afternoon of "surf swimming" in this romanticized engraving dating from the 1870s.

part of festivals (like Makahiki) and community-building activities. Hawaiian royalty, or *ali'i*, even had special surfboards that only they could ride, and wave breaks reserved for them (commoners could be put to death for surfing *ali'i* boards or spots).

First glimpses from the outside

In 1778 celebrated British sea captain James Cook and his crew encountered the Hawaiian Islands during a third discovery mission across the Pacific Ocean. Soon after mooring at Kealakekua Bay on the Kona Coast of the "Big Island," Cook and his men saw the locals paddling and surfing on solid wood boards. The Europeans had seen similar swell-powered feats accomplished in canoes while in Tahiti, and such a sight was famously recorded by Cook in his ship's journal, in a passage (quoted in the foreword to this book) in which he writes about having witnessed a local man riding the waves, and the palpable pleasure to be derived from such a natural activity.

But Cook and his crew did not view people standing up while riding waves, in the style we would recognize today, but rather kneeling or lying on their boards. Descriptions of surfboard riding appear in Cook's voyage logs, along with early illustrations of men and women surfers. When Cook was killed before he left Hawaii, Lieutenant James King continued to document information about the fantastic island chain and spoke of the wave-riding natives he witnessed. Back in Europe, the journal of Cook's final voyage was published and word of these surfing islanders spread across the continent and into newly independent America.

Western influences

The next contact between Hawaiians and westerners had less to do with exploration and more to do with religion. Thirty years after Cook's arrival, European and American missionaries came to Hawaii, intent on converting the natives, with their ancient, atavistic customs. The missionaries objected to Hawaiian culture in several ways, particularly the people's polytheistic beliefs and casual nudity. They thought Hawaiians weren't industrious enough, believing that they spent too much time on festivals, games, and surfing.

Throughout the rest of the 1800s, these English-speaking proselytizers erected settlements across the islands, established a strict theocracy, forced the locals to dress modestly, and halted what they believed to be a lascivious mixing of the sexes. Surfing itself was not directly outlawed, but the activity's popularity waned as the once deeply rooted religious and cultural celebrations, which centered on surfing, were discouraged. By the turn of the twentieth century, only residents of small enclaves still rode surfboards, and the practice of surfing was at its lowest point in the islands' history. Some estimate that just fifty Hawaiians, mostly on the island of Oahu, in and around Waikiki, practiced the ancient sport. Most surfers simply rode on their knees or belly, and the wooden boards they used were markedly less sophisticated than those that had been carefully produced centuries before. Nevertheless, surfing was on the brink of a modern revival.

Above In this nineteenth-century image a Hawaiian holding an *alaia* and wearing only a *malo* poses in front of Diamond Head.

Surfing takes off

The pure sport of surfing received a powerful shove from several hands as the twentieth century dawned. One of the key figures in the modern promotion of surfing and the wonders of Waikiki was an American southerner named Alexander Hume Ford. An adventurer and newspaperman, Ford stopped in Hawaii during a sailing excursion to Australia and ended up staying.

Immediately taken with surfing, he made a board, and practiced incessantly. The fervent and zestful Ford set about helping to spread the word about his new homeland and surfboard riding, and he energetically encouraged Waikiki visitors to experience surfing. He then penned a surfing article for *Collier* magazine, creating a bit of mainstream buzz about this unique sport. A savvy marketer, Ford knew opportunity when he saw it. In 1907 acclaimed author Jack London was vacationing on Oahu's south shore, and Ford urged London to attempt riding waves. Despite the fact he never actually stood up on a board, the experience of paddling through the breakers and getting rolled by churning white water excited London immensely. In a lengthy article about his experiences with the glorious Hawaiian sport for *Woman's Home Companion* magazine, London wrote a poetic narrative offered by a humbled, reverential narrator. Within, London describes his Waikiki surfing instructor as "a brown Mercury." "His heels are winged," London continues, "and in them is the swiftness of the sea." The piece was later republished in his 1911 travel tale *The Cruise of the Snark*, and London's flattering account intrigued a worldwide audience.

Ford's assistance in establishing Waikiki's Outrigger Canoe Club in 1908, though, may have been his biggest contribution to the sport he loved. This was surfing's first officially chartered organization, and its mission was to help revive the Hawaiian traditions of riding waves on surfboards and paddling swift outrigger canoes. The club

Below Tourists take an exciting ride inside an outrigger canoe as a slew of locals share the wave along Waikiki Beach.

was a place where surfers and paddlers, mostly haole, or Caucasians, could congregate, store their equipment, compete, and preserve the ancient art.

Roll up, roll up, and see the show

By 1908 Irish Hawaiian surfer George Freeth, London's "Brown Mercury," was starring in spectacular, one-man surfing demonstrations in Southern California. Hired by railroad magnate Henry E. Huntington to demonstrate the amazing stunt of "walking on water," as well as other Hawaiian sports, Freeth performed the stunt of riding onto the beach while standing upright on a solid wood board. Huntington's aim was to publicize his new Pacific Electric Red Car railway line and the terminus of its Los Angeles–Redondo route–the saltwater plunge pool at Redondo Beach. The gimmick succeeded. Freeth's 1907 and 1908 surfboard-riding shows attracted thousands to Redondo, Venice, and Huntington beaches, and to coastal spots beyond. The earliest wave of California surfers took to the ocean in the months directly following Freeth's historic surfing demonstrations, in what was the beginning of the modern-day popularity of the sport outside of Hawaii.

Meanwhile, the sport was gaining ground in Hawaii as well. A second surf club, Hui Nalu, whose membership was mainly Hawaiian and more athletic, was officially chartered in 1911 after six years of loose affiliation. At the heart of Hui Nalu was one of its cofounders and finest surfers, a young local named Duke Paoa Kahanamoku.

Kahanamoku, an outstanding swimmer, had broken multiple world records and was invited to represent the United States at the 1912 Olympic Games in Stockholm, Sweden. On his return trip, bearing gold and silver swimming medals, he introduced surfboard riding at American East Coast beaches. During the following few years, Kahanamoku put on demonstrations in California, Australia, and New Zealand.

Kahanamoku's wave-riding showcases were impressive, but the manner in which he presented the act–with the charisma of a world-class athlete and a global Hawaiian ambassador–gave a regal face to the sport. When home on Oahu, Kahanamoku was a celebrated star, welcomed as a member of the glitterati in his hometown of Waikiki. Duke Kahanamoku was the most famous surfer of his day and remains the most influential surfer ever. Bronze statues of him stand in Hawaii and Australia, and he is the only surfer to have been featured on a U.S. Postal Service stamp, testament to his title of "Father of Modern Surfing."

The first surf tourist hits Hawaii

As a teenager, Wisconsin-born Tom Blake, who would become one of the country's legendary surfers, was greatly influenced by Duke Kahanamoku. At the age of about ten, Blake watched a newsreel of Hawaiians surfing at Waikiki, and the footage piqued the youngster's interest. Purely by chance, a few years later, in 1920, Blake met Kahanamoku in a Detroit theater lobby, where Kahanamoku and some of his Olympic teammates had stopped to view the movie reel of his recent gold medal swimming victory in Antwerp, Belgium. Kahanamoku offered Blake a firm handshake and an offhand invitation to visit Waikiki, which Blake took seriously. Blake soon moved to Southern California and tried surfing in Santa Monica the following year, but suffered a bad wipeout during his first effort and didn't try again for several weeks. In 1924, though, while working as a lifeguard, Blake re-encountered Kahanamoku, who was living in Los Angeles part-time, and the two became friends. Later in the year Blake finally visited Hawaii–making history as the first person to travel to these islands specifically to surf. He was one of the few haole surfers to be fully accepted by the tight-knit Waikiki beachboy crew and was even voted into the locals-only Hui Nalu club.

New boards speed faster and lighter

Blake stayed in Hawaii for less than a year on his first trip. During that time, he studied the surfboard collection at Honolulu's Bishop Museum and decided to build a fifteen-foot replica paddleboard of an eighteenth-century olo, the longest of ancient Hawaiian surfboards. Eager for his wooden board to dry properly, he drilled a series of holes through the board to speed the process,

Right Olympic gold-medal swimmer, unofficial Ambassador of Aloha, and "The Father of Modern Surfing," Duke Kahanamoku.

then covered the deck and bottom with thin sheets of marine plywood. What Blake had done in the process was to make the board lighter, thereby producing the first major improvement in surfboard design. (Up to this point, surfboards weighed between seventy-five and one hundred pounds.)

Initially, Blake's odd-looking board was ridiculed, but the laughing stopped when he rode it in the surf and, later, smashed local paddleboard racing records. Blake refined his "hollow board," or "kookbox," design over the next few years, and the end result was a cigar-shaped board, pointed at both ends, with a chambered frame and layers of thin, hardwood veneer on the outside to seal it, in all weighing far less than the solid wood, plank-style boards that had reigned since ancient times.

However, the ever-ingenious surfer from Wisconsin didn't rest on his laurels. Between 1926 and 1937, Blake introduced keel fins to the tails of boards, and patented his hollow surfboards and paddleboards–both major innovations. He was the first to have his boards manufactured on a large scale and also created the first waterproof camera housing for surf photography–he published his shots in *National Geographic.* Blake wrote the first book about surfing, *Hawaiian Surfriders 1935*, and submitted a pair of do-it-yourself surfboard-building articles to *Popular Mechanics* and *Popular Science*. Indisputably, Tom Blake was the twentieth century's greatest surf innovator.

By the early 1940s, surfing's roots outside of Hawaii had taken hold, and surf clubs were formed in places like Australia, California, Peru, and South Africa. Plank surfboards, as well as Blake-style hollows, were the

Left Innovative surfer Tom Blake stands in front of a lineup of some of the surf- and paddle-boards crafted by him in this classic photograph, circa 1930.

period's only board types, and any further innovation was essentially halted by the onset of war. Surfing in the mainland United States and Hawaii virtually disappeared as a pastime when a vast number of American youth joined the Allied fight in World War II. At the same time, however, American GIs were helping to introduce the sport to some European and African countries while they were stationed overseas.

A new surfing generation

After the war, materials and aerodynamic theories previously used mainly for military purposes were desensitized, and proved to be a driving force behind the next wave of surfboard evolution. Inspired by Blake's pioneering spirit, a new generation began to experiment with board shapes and construction methods. As a result, surfboards were dramatically overhauled during the next twenty years.

In the first surfboard design advancement since Blake's innovation in the 1920s, now lightweight balsa wood boards were being encased within waterproof cocoons of resin-saturated fiberglass cloth. By the end of the 1940s, polyurethane foam surfboard cores had replaced balsa, sources of which had become scarce, and became the norm. As foam and fiberglass boards were refined in the 1950s, Malibu surpassed Waikiki as the sport's cultural focal point and testing ground. Los Angeles-based board builders like Greg Noll, Joe Quigg, Bob Simmons, and Dale Velzy, assisted by these new materials and techniques, shaped lightweight boards that averaged ten feet in length, turned and handled well, and could be carried to the water's edge far more easily than their weighty predecessors.

Manageable surfboards most definitely helped to make the sport more accessible and appealing to the masses, and they played an important part in the first great surfing boom. However, the boom was also the result of other factors. Boards were now sold in surf shops and via mail order, and a marketable surf industry was coming into its own.

People were inspired to learn the sport from watching the newest surf movies by pioneers like Bud Browne and John Severson. And, maybe most important, a pop culture phenomenon called "Gidget" really helped break the whole scene wide open. Based on the true-life tales of his teenage daughter's adventures in Malibu during the mid-1950s, Frederick Kohner's popular 1957 novel, *Gidget: The Little Girl with Big Ideas*, and the feel-good Hollywood movie version that followed, fostered a sense that surfing was now hip, young, and fun. It seemed the perfect escape for a generation trying to turn the page on not one, but two, horrific wars (the Korean War had followed World War II just a few years later).

Below Vacationers relax on the beach at Waikiki in the early 1950s; Oahu was becoming more widely known as a beach paradise.

Surfing heroes

Surfing in the 1960s rode the wave of innovations from the previous decade, as longboard shapes were refined and surf colonies sprang up around the globe. Peak performance styles of the day, like "hotdogging" and nose riding, were demonstrated at the world's best breaks by a talented international surfing contingent.

The decade also marked the introduction of intense surf travel. A worldwide search for undiscovered waves in every temperate region (inspired by Bruce Brown's masterpiece surf travel movie, *The Endless Summer*) was on, and surfers sifted through uncharted regions ranging from Africa and Europe to Central and South America. The sport's influence, too, was rising to new levels. The first surf magazines were printed, surf music appeared (a style exemplified by the electric guitar riffs of Dick Dale and his slew of surf-themed albums), and surf-wear manufacturers capitalized on the sport's popularity by creating mass-produced trunks and logo T-shirts. Hollywood pumped out hordes of corny "waxploitation" beach party flicks, and some of the first professional surfers (led by Phil Edwards) were getting paid to ride waves.

Competition gets serious

It was only fitting, then, that competitive associations were formed and major contests held to showcase the world's finest surfers. In Hawaii, contests such as Oahu's Makaha International and Duke Kahanamoku Invitational (at Sunset Beach) were the premier annual gatherings, establishing a competitive benchmark that paired the best surfers on Earth with powerful waves.

Contests also gained popularity outside of Hawaii. The first sanctioned series of surfing World Championships truly mirrored the sport's global presence. At the 1964 world contest, held at Manly Beach in Sydney, Australia, local Bernard "Midget" Farrelly took top honors, and the second world title was won by Peruvian Felipe Pomar the following year.

In 1966 contestants from around the world came to San Diego, California, for the third world championship. And, as had occurred the first year, the crown was worn by an Aussie, this time thanks to a "total involvement" type of surfing–personified by winner Robert "Nat" Young–that countered the nose-ride-focused trend of the day and instead featured critical and powerful turns in the pocket, or curl, of a wave.

Surfboard designs entered a new and exciting age as the sun set on the 1960s, driven by a growing list of worldwide high-performance breaks that were a far cry

The Coronado Surf Club from San Diego, California, gathers at North Beach for a group portrait—baggies, woodie wagons, surfboards, and all.

from the gentle waves found at Waikiki or Malibu. In the process, a new era of surfing was begun by Robert "Nat" Young, shaper Bob McTavish, and California knee-boarder George Greenough.

The shortboard revolution

By the early 1970s, the cumbersome, nine- and ten-foot surfboards were virtual dinosaurs, nudged out by shorter, more maneuverable, sleeker shapes. In this time known as the "shortboard revolution," experimental boards, running from useful to useless, logical to ludicrous, were tooled and tested in an effort to turn harder, move faster, and maintain control inside the tube.

This was a critical decade of surfboard advancements, with experimental shapers building space-age watercraft, contours, fins, and rail edges in both backyards and factories alike. Designs like Ben Aipa's stinger, Steve Lis's swallowtail keel fish, the Campbell brothers' bonzer, and Michael Hynson's down rail speed boards pushed the limits of the psychedelic era, with shapers like McTavish and Hawaii's Dick Brewer leading the charge.

Armed with a bevy of boards that performed well in demanding conditions, intrepid surfers led another push to find flawless spots beyond the known surf map. The goal of riding the biggest waves, most evident between the late 1930s and 1970, was now replaced by the hunt for hollow, perfectly-foiled waves. In Hawaii, all focus zoomed in to Oahu's north shore, specifically Pipeline. The famed beautiful caverns of Banzai Pipeline became the measuring stick against which all other waves were judged. Islands off Africa, Europe, and Asia were explored by a hardy group of international surfers and shown to hold many of the world's most majestic waves. Most of these exotic discoveries were eventually featured in surf magazines and surf films, alerting the rest of the surfing population to what lay at the end of bumpy roads and boat excursions. Crude camps catering exclusively to surfers were even erected in some remote regions, starting with the all-inclusive, jungle-rimmed "surf resort" at Grajagan in Java, Indonesia.

The early 1980s once again signaled a shift in surfing style. The twin-fin-propelled, sweeping, down-the-line carves and "rip, tear, and lacerate" ideals (epitomized by world champion Mark Richards of Australia, winner of four consecutive titles between 1979 and 1982, and mimicked by both pros and regular Joes) remained the touchstone of performance as the 1970s ended. But in 1981 a new design by local Simon Anderson, unveiled at Bell's Beach Surf Classic, turned the entire surfboard industry on its ear. The board Anderson rode to victory

Below By the 1970s, Pipeline had become the focal point for surfers everywhere. An unidentified slider takes his single-fin through the world's most famous bowl.

at Bell's was propelled by a triangular cluster of three fins at the tail. Although three-finned boards had been experimented with in the previous decade, Anderson's "tri-fin," or "thruster," configuration incorporated three fins of the same size across a wide square tail, producing unmatched drive and stability. Over the next few seasons, many professionals converted to thrusters, and a fresh, "shredding" style of surfing was born.

The 1980s explosion

Competitive surfing's governing body, too, was changing. In 1982 International Professional Surfers, founded in 1968 by Fred Hemmings, was replaced by Ian Cairns's new Association of Surfing Professionals (ASP) due to an allegedly overriding sentiment that pro surfing wasn't evolving properly. The format of a global cumulative-point men and women's tour remained, but some venues changed, more events were added, bigger sponsors signed on, and, indeed, prize purses grew. As the popularity of the ASP and its constituents grew throughout the 1980s, so did the giant surf-wear companies. Pros posing in fluorescent-colored garb for magazine advertisements guided the industry's staggering growth and pushed profit margins of major manufacturers into the mega millions.

The 1980s also signified the return of two nearly forgotten facets of the sport: longboarding and big-wave surfing. As baby-boomer surfers began to reach middle age, the shortboards cornering the market were just too small and dysfunctional for many of them, causing some to dig up old longboards and shapers to develop a lightweight, newfangled, modern longboard. Big-wave riding also returned to prominence with a giant boost by the "Quiksilver in Memory of Eddie Aikau" contest at Waimea Bay, the first competition of its kind. Held in honor of a legendary Hawaiian lifeguard and big-wave rider who tragically died in 1978, the event would only be run if the waves were twenty feet or larger. The 1986 "Eddie" welcomed thirty of the planet's best big-wave

Below The vast crowd on hand to catch the 1986 Op Pro surf contest at Huntington Beach—prior to the infamous police clash.

surfers, which is still protocol, and was won by Eddie's brother Clyde Aikau. Four years later, the next time the waves grew large enough to hold it, a $55,000 winner's check, the richest purse ever for a single contest, was handed to Keone Downing, son of revered big-wave pioneer and event director George Downing. Today, the "Eddie" is the most respected big-wave contest on Earth.

A sport that never stands still

Surfing progressed into the new millennium with a new momentum and surge of popularity. The ASP circuit gained audiences and funding, and surfboard and soft-goods manufacturing became a billion-dollar industry. Surf schools, wave-forecasting Web sites, and a thriving apparel industry recruited beginners of all ages to the sport. All the while, advanced wet-suit technology allowed surfers to expand the surf map into bitter-cold regions like Iceland, Norway, and Russia. Most notably, the boom was assisted by a blossoming women's market triggered by Quiksilver's Roxy clothing line for young women and the exceptional surfing ability of four-time world champion Lisa Andersen, the face of Roxy.

Quiksilver's other major '90s commodity was Kelly Slater, who mastered a futuristic set of moves on Al Merrick's anemically thin shortboard thruster designs. His popularity crossed over into pop culture, as he played a recurring role on the international television hit *Baywatch* and engaged in a well-publicized relationship with its star, Pamela Anderson. A world champion nine times over (and still counting as of publication), Slater and the rest of the "New School" surfers, sometimes called the "Momentum" generation–a group whose insane talents were shown in Taylor Steele's *Momentum* surf videos–changed the sport with an exciting, next-century style of surfing that included fins-free, tail-sliding maneuvers, ridiculous tube riding, and giant aerials.

Above The inimitable professional with freakish talent, Kelly Slater, celebrates winning his sixth world title.

Beyond the shore, a subsport emerged in 1992. Tow-in surfing, where riders holding water-ski ropes are pulled and swung into behemoth waves by partners driving personal watercraft, was immediately thrust to the forefront of surfing, completely redefining big waves and big-wave surfboards. Monster waves found from Hawaii to Ireland have been conquered thanks to tow-in surfing.

Surfing is now a menagerie of styles, from shredding shortboards through hollow walls and nose-riding longboards across small waves, to reviving retro board theories. The sport has matured to include every wave-lapped corner of the globe, and surf images abound in film and advertising. Practiced by people of every race, income, age, and credo, surfing is truly a global culture.

Above Longboard pro Belinda Peterson-Baggs, exemplifying the grace and beauty associated with women's surfing.

Great surf collections

Surfing has been practiced for more than a millennium, but it is only recently that people began collecting and archiving its historical artifacts and recording the sport's evolutionary timeline. Here is just a handful of the many museums dedicated to documenting the story of surfing and bringing its colorful history vividly to life.

CALIFORNIA SURF MUSEUM

The California Surf Museum (CSM) was the first dedicated nonprofit museum to capture the culture and heritage of surfing. CSM is the brainchild of Stuart Resor, Ian Urquhart, Don Fine, Jane Schmauss, Kevin Kinnear, Catherine Woolsey, and June Cocheles and now one of the most respected surf resource centers in the world. Until it opened in 1986 little had been done in an organized way to preserve the history of the sport.

The CSM collection chronicles the state's rich surfing past in the context of a global history, and attracts tens of thousands of visitors each year with exhibits such as surfboards from the early 1900s to today; photographs; and memorabilia like classic shaping tools, bathing suits, posters, and trophies. Online, visit www.surfmuseum.org.

INTERNATIONAL SURFING MUSEUM

The International Surfing Museum (ISM) began as an effort to save the disappearing surf history of Huntington Beach, California, spearheaded by founder Natalie Kotsch, a local teacher and antique shop owner. But it was soon agreed that the focus should be broader, incorporating surfing's worldwide past. Originally located

Left and this page Thanks to a global family of surf museums and foundations, historical artifacts like an antique solid wood board and one of the earliest known surf photographs will forever be preserved for future generations to view.

in a tiny storefront near the pier, ISM moved in 1990 to a larger facility, in the heart of the downtown beach scene. Here you will find the Surfing Walk of Fame, a sidewalk alongside the Pacific Coast Highway celebrating many of the sport's important contributors. Inside ISM, exhibits chart the development of the sport and its counterculture, including a bronze bust of Duke Kahanamoku, the Bolex camera Bruce Brown used to film *The Endless Summer*, and surf music legend Dick Dale's first electric guitar. The facility also includes a theater that runs vintage surf movies. See www.surfingmuseum.org.

SURFING HERITAGE FOUNDATION

The Surfing Heritage Foundation (SHF), in San Clemente, California, is the work of founder Dick Metz and respected collector Spencer Croul. SHF opened its amazing archive to the public in 2005, after several years' existence in a private warehouse. SHF houses an extraordinary colletion of more than 150 pristine boards, displayed chronologically, with another 300 or so held in storage and rotated in as needed. Behind the scenes, SHF is leading the way in digitally archiving historical surfing memorabilia like print photographs, oral records, video interviews, scrapbooks, and more. For more information go online and visit www.surfingheritage.com.

SURF WORLD

Australia's Surf World, in Torquay, Victoria, is the largest surf and beach culture museum on the planet, with nearly 1,200 square feet (365 sq m) of space dedicated to the continent's surfing heritage and leading figures. Founded in 1993 by Victorian native and pioneer surfer Peter Troy with the help of friends Vic Tantau and Al Reid, the group recognized a need to preserve Australia's surfing history and aimed to provide a place to share one of the world's most exhilarating activities and lifestyles.

A shrine to the Australian chapters within the larger surf story, Surf World has a movie theater; a complete, live shaping bay where professionals show crowds how surfboards are created; nearly 200 surfboards on display, including some ridden by legends such as Duke Kahanamoku, Michael Peterson, Terry Fitzgerald, Mark Occhilupo, and Kelly Slater; and even a surf culture installation filled with period memorabilia and a full-size, walk-through Volkswagen Kombi van. To learn more, visit www.surfworld.org.au.

THE BERNICE P. BISHOP MUSEUM

The Bernice P. Bishop Museum, in Honolulu, Oahu, is Hawaii's oldest and largest. Started by Charles Reed Bishop in memory of his wife, a member of Hawaiian royalty, the museum dates back to 1889. Bishop is a wondrous repository of Pacific, Polynesian, and Hawaiian natural and cultural history. Though it is not a surf-specific museum, it does have the oldest known archive of surfboards and surfing-related objects. Here, many of the world's rarest surfboards reside, including ancient boards from the late 1700s and some that belonged to the *ali'i*, Hawaiian royalty. Also represented in the collection are early kookboxes by Tom Blake, a vintage John Kelly hot curl, items of Duke Kahanamoku's personal belongings, classic photographs by Charles Gurrey, and early movies. For more information on the museum visit www.bishopmuseum.org.

Top A rare 1920s image of Australians posing at Lorn Beach. **Center** Bruce Brown's Bolex camera; using just this one camera, he filmed his masterpiece, *The Endless Summer*. **Bottom** Built-to-scale models show the evolution of surfboards, from ancient to present times.

No matter where you live, the chances are that surfable waves exist only a short flight or a road trip away. With a little research and the desire to discover the surf spots that best suit the individual, every wave type, crowd factor, and condition can be found on "Planet Surf." There is a big, blue marble out there—the joy and learning benefit for the surfer is in experimenting with what this watery world has to offer.

Planet Surf

The big picture

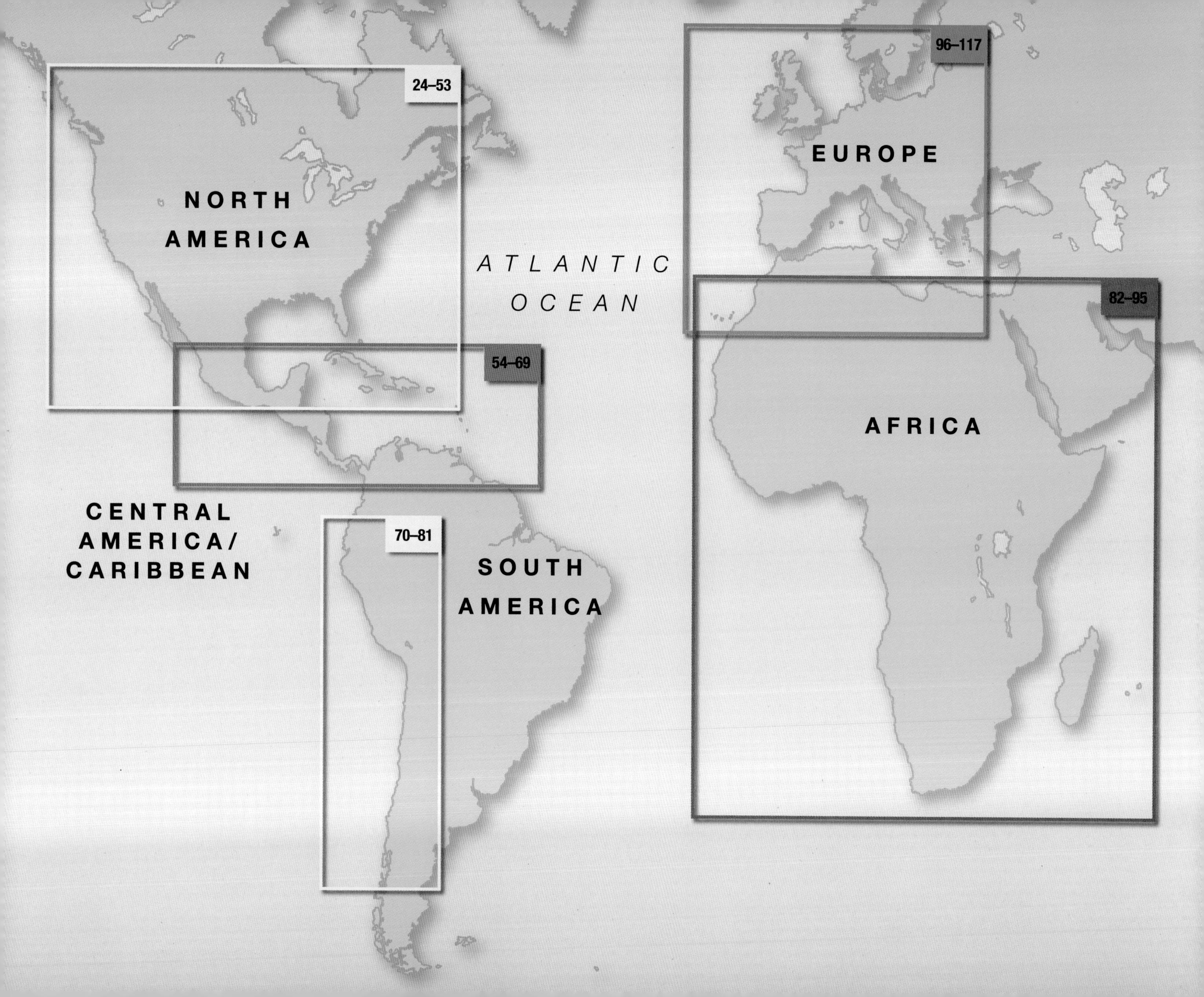

24–53
NORTH
AMERICA
ATLANTIC
OCEAN
54–69
CENTRAL
AMERICA/
CARIBBEAN
70–81
SOUTH
AMERICA
96–117
EUROPE
82–95
AFRICA

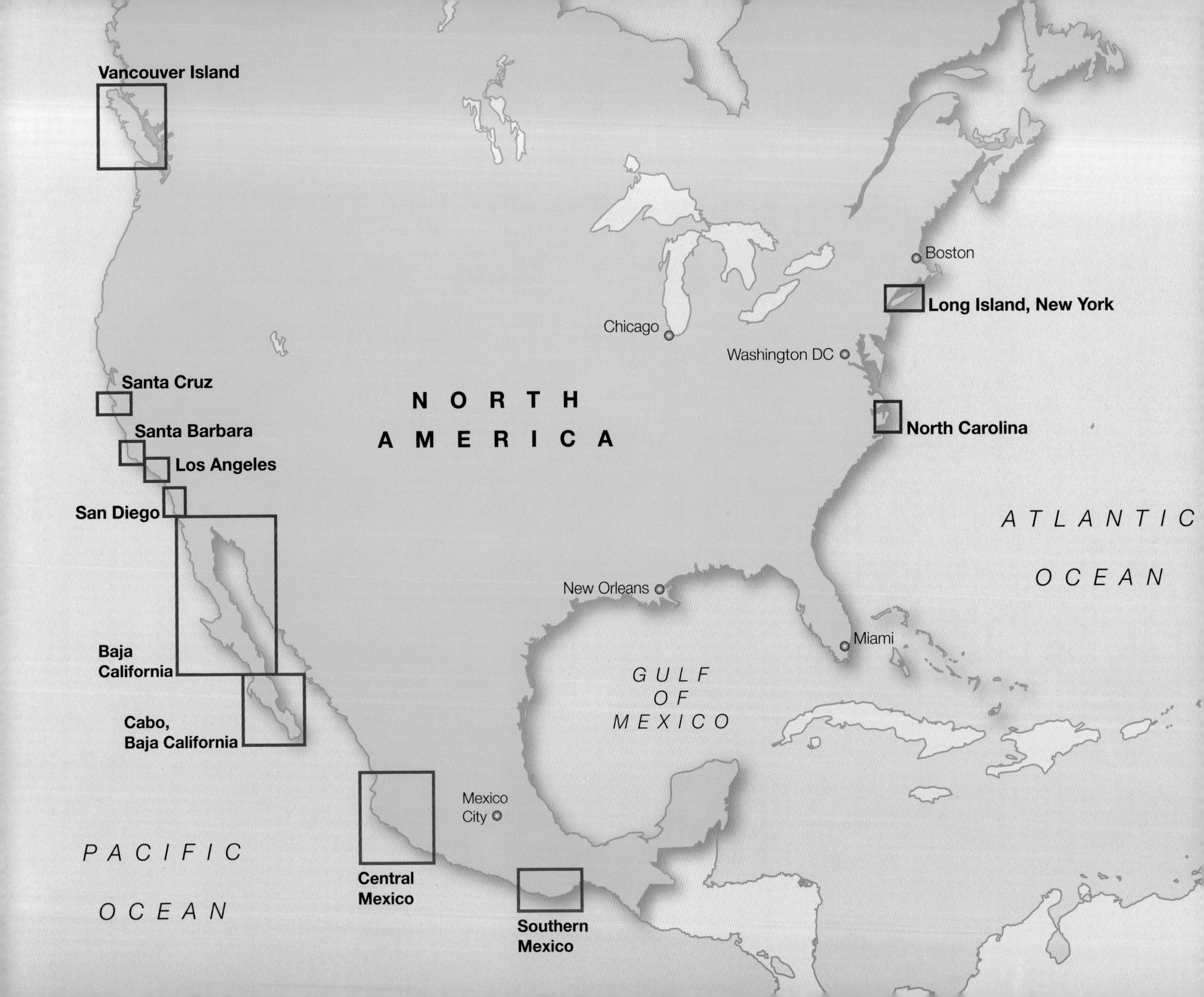

Vancouver Island
Boston
Long Island, New York
Chicago
Washington DC
Santa Cruz
NORTH
AMERICA
North Carolina
Santa Barbara
Los Angeles
San Diego
ATLANTIC
OCEAN
New Orleans
Miami
Baja
California
GULF
OF
MEXICO
Cabo,
Baja California
Mexico
City
PACIFIC
OCEAN
Central
Mexico
Southern
Mexico

North America

North America has three distinct mainland coastlines containing several thousand miles of beachfront. Kept busy by two vast oceans, not to mention the Gulf of Mexico and the Caribbean Sea, and with wave zones as different as Alaska and Mexico, it is little wonder that more than 2.5 million surfers call North America home.

Canada, Washington, Oregon, and California face the North Pacific Ocean and receive a steady stream of winter swells and a handful of massive low-pressure systems onto the western shore. In summertime the West Coast also accepts swells from the southern hemisphere. On the flip side, Canada, Nova Scotia, and the entire eastern seaboard of the United States are dealt wave offerings from the stormy North Atlantic Ocean as well as hurricanes generated from as far afield as Africa. In the south, Gulf States such as Texas and Alabama see rideable surf from these seasonal, tropical storms. Freshwater, wind-borne waves can even be found on some of the Great Lakes.

The art of surfboard riding has been a North American practice and culture for more than a century, and the sheer number of surfers in North America tops that found in any other region. At the end of the 1920s, you could likely have counted the number of surfers here on your fingers and toes. Nowadays, it can be difficult to find an empty parking spot or peak along the thousands of wave-riddled coastal miles. Overcrowded waves are a major concern for surfers in North America, and the dearth of empty waves has spawned an ugly epidemic of localism that sometimes turns nasty.

Population and urban expanse along much of North America's coastline contributes to the world's number one hazard for surfers: polluted run-off. Everything from oil and agricultural pesticides to trash and killer diseases are funneled into the oceans through rivers, treatment plants, and sewer systems. If any good has stemmed from this grave problem, it is the establishment of watchdog organizations such as the Surfrider Foundation, Respect the Beach, and Blue Water Task Force, not to mention the many grassroots groups working to improve their local water quality.

Vancouver Island

Long Beach, River Jordan, Cox Bay, China Beach

Located in Canada's extreme southwest, Vancouver Island is a must for any traveling surfer's wish list. With verdant mountains, snowcapped peaks, craggy offshore islands, and old-growth forests providing a backdrop, plus a coastline ripe with possibility but short on expert surfers, Vancouver Island is a bountiful place for hardy and well-prepared wave hunters to explore, and a beautiful locale for beginners to get acclimated.

The town of Tofino is the nation's surfing center, and, during summer, when the region's waves are generally weak, thousands of novice surfers take to the nearby easy beach breaks. As both the water and air temperatures drop in autumn, though, much of the crowd clears out and early winter wave patterns begin to push in favorable west and northwest swells. True winter is best avoided here, unless whitecaps, giant storm surf, and torrential rain are your idea of fun. Spring usually brings hit-or-miss conditions but often produces a few of the better days in the year.

The southern half of Vancouver Island has a variety of surf spots that range from easily accessible to downright difficult to find. Starting inside the Juan de Fuca Strait, the waves at River Jordan, The Point, Port Renfrew, and China Beach get good swells that can wrap into the waterway. North, near Tofino and Ucluelet, the southwest-facing coastline receives more consistent surf but can get crowded at places such as Long Beach and Cox Bay when the conditions are good.

The real allure of Vancouver Island is that it's an unexplored surf frontier. While beaches near the coastal towns and along the highway are the main surf hubs, most of the island remains remote, and there are high-quality waves to be discovered beyond thick forests, down remote logging roads, and along the myriad tiny, offshore islets that fringe the northern end. Of course, finding such deserted waves might require a good four-wheel-drive vehicle, a sturdy boat, and some local knowledge, but true adventure awaits in Vancouver Island, and that is something worth cherishing these days.

Left Sometimes just walking to the waves can be a colder experience than the frigid water itself.

Surf Vancouver Island

Location:
Pacific Ocean

Country:
Canada

Language:
English and French

Currency:
Canadian Dollar

The Good . . .
- Secret spots
- Summertime beginner beaches
- Open surf frontier

And the Bad . . .
- Difficult access
- Cold water
- Black bears
- Wolves
- Territorial locals

VANCOUVER ISLAND
Vancouver
Tofino
Ucluelet
Strait of Juan de Fuca

Key to map
- Cox Bay
- Long Beach
- Port Renfrew
- China Beach
- The Point
- River Jordan

Right Cold, clean, and pristine are the best words to describe surfing on Vancouver Island. This is an incredible place for an off-the-beaten-path surf trip.

One of the gems in the crown of Santa Cruz surf is Mitchell's Cove. Santa Cruz is chock full of wave options—from powerful to playful, packed to unoccupied.

Santa Cruz

Steamer Lane, The Harbor, Pleasure Point

California's true "Surf City," Santa Cruz lies at the northern end of a half-circle arc of coastline sweeping around Monterey Bay. With a wide-open swell window that accepts both summertime souths as well as raw, wintertime juice from the north, this area is known for its great variety of consistent surf, world-class point breaks, beautiful scenery, and hordes of talented surfers.

Santa Cruz is also steeped in surf history. Legend has it that the first surfers to ride waves in California, the three Hawaiian-born Kawananakoa brothers, did so here in 1885; Jack O'Neill created some of the earliest surfing wetsuits after moving his shop to the area around 1959; the surf leash was invented by a couple of locals in 1970;

Key to map

- Four Mile
- Natural Bridges
- Steamer Lane
- The Harbor
- San Lorenzo River
- Pleasure Point
- The Hook
- Capitola River Mouth

Below A flock of locals of the feathered variery oversees a winter scene at Natural Bridges.

Surf Santa Cruz

Location:
Pacific Ocean

Country:
United States of America

Language:
English

Currency:
US Dollar

The Good . . .

- World-class waves
- Many wave options
- Year-round surf

And the Bad . . .

- Cold water
- Crowds
- Sharks

and surfing's aerial-style roots, which began with Kevin Reed in the late 1970s, are planted in Santa Cruz.

The real deal in Santa Cruz is in town. Separated into west and east sections by more than just name, this once-sleepy area is a true surfer's playground. To the east of Santa Cruz Harbor lies a stellar run of high-quality waves, including Little Windansea, Pleasure Point, The Hook, Sharks Cove, and Capitola River Mouth. Pleasure Point is the major east side player, with long, clean, playful, right-hand walls beneath sandstone bluffs that have sections to satisfy both shortboarders and longboarders, from gremmies to salty dogs. Nearby is The Harbor, a mutant, sucking, sandbar barrel that is technically illegal to surf, but is nonetheless ridden–and often.

Moving westward the visitor can find the fickle but occasionally impressive rights and lefts formed at the mouth of the San Lorenzo River, reportedly the first spot surfed by the Kawananakoas. Farther west is one of the most crowded and competitive lineups in all of North America: the world-famous Steamer Lane.

The Lane's situation on the coast protects it from all but the nastiest onshore winds, and its heavy kelp forests also help groom the surface. Steamer Lane begins at the lighthouse with the Point section, peaking up into meaty, hollow rights on medium to low tides. Then comes the Slot, a steep drop with high-performance walls that start in a nook alongside the bluff. Next, the three reefs of Middle Peak offer sloping rights and better lefts that shift around according to swell size and direction; these reefs are capable of holding some of winter's biggest waves. Finally, at the inside edge of Middle Peak sits Indicators, a good, point-break-style right-hander that welcomes a thick crop of surfers when it's at its best. Legendary swells have been known to produce thrilling rides nearly a mile long when all four sections of The Lane connect.

Above The Harbor breaks intimidatingly close to the breakwall, and with the thick lip comes dark water and a black hole of glory. Nobody was willing to roll the dice on this mean one.

Right A rainy and stormy Christmas Day gives way to a brief moment of rainbow bliss during sunset at The Hook.

The northern end of Santa Cruz County holds a handful of fun beach breaks and reefs worth checking out when the crowds in "town" become intolerable. Explore the sandbars at Waddell and Scott Creeks, the left-hand, boiling reef at Davenport Landing, the high-grade point break found four miles outside of Santa Cruz city limits that is inventively named Four Mile, and the heavy, bowling rights at Natural Bridges.

South of town is also considered a good escape destination when you're looking for some empty water, although the waves are generally smaller than those found up north. The fifteen miles of fun beaches that stretch from Capitola down to Moss Landing offer respite and several more chances for stellar waves, but the area is without much reef bottom.

Santa Barbara

The Ranch, El Capitan, Sandspit, Rincon del Mar

Surf Santa Barbara

Location:
Pacific Ocean
Country:
United States of America
Language:
English
Currency:
US Dollar

The Good . . .
- World-class points
- Wave variety

And the Bad . . .
- Small to flat in summer
- Crowds
- Limited swell windows

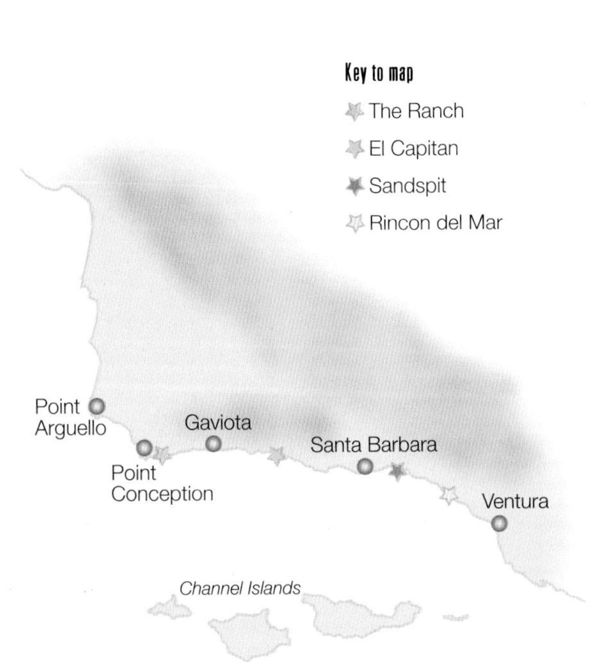

Santa Barbara is a unique product of geography and swell windows. With its south-facing shores, you might think that southern hemisphere waves would turn on this land of right-hand reefs and points. However, several of the Channel Islands below, which also have rideable surf, block nearly any south or southwest swell. Contrarily, on the northern end, Point Arguello and Point Conception jut so far west that direct north swells are reduced, skirting the entire county. When good west and northwest waves squeeze through the islands' passes and into that limited swell window, though, the normally dormant breaks of Santa Barbara spring to life, luring surfers from all directions with a sweet siren song.

Below The mutant waves at Sandspit, in Santa Barbara Harbor, need a solid west swell even to begin breaking. But with sufficient juice, it can set up into what many claim is one of the longest tubes in the state.

Reaching from Conception to Gaviota, The Ranch is a dreamy yet difficult-to-access run of famous waves on fourteen miles of privately owned and jealously guarded coast, kept under lock and key. You must either be invited onto The Ranch or make the lengthy journey by boat to surf here and then deal with the locals. However, a classic day at The Ranch can provide a glittering page for the memory book.

One of the many state park campgrounds in the county includes the rare waves at El Capitan, a fickle break capable of flawless, dredging, hollow rights on big west swells. In town, Sandspit, a shallow sandbar in Santa Barbara Harbor, is a manmade work of art. When it works (which, in truth, is not that often), Sandspit backwashes into a fast, churning, ripping barrel ride that many claim to be California's longest.

At least twenty other high-quality spots exist in and around Santa Barbara, but its southernmost point, found on the county line shared with Ventura, garners the most attention. Rincon del Mar, also known as the Queen of the Coast, is often called the state's best wave. A world-famous right-hand point break, first surfed by Gates Foss in the late 1930s, Rincon's cobblestone reef, river mouth, and seasonal sandbars send perfectly formed waves around the entire point, from Indicator to The Cove. The results? Achingly long, supersonic-speed walls with round tube sections that can offer mind-numbing rides that will leave your legs quivering.

Below A priceless and breathtaking view of The Ranch, usually only afforded to the fortunate residents of the private coastal region and those boating in toward the shore at precisely the right time.

Key to map

- Leo Carrillo
- Malibu
- Topanga Point
- El Porto
- Manhattan
- Hermosa Beach
- Redondo Beach
- Indicator
- Lunada Bay

Los Angeles

Leo Carrillo, Malibu, El Porto, Palos Verdes

Surf Los Angeles

Location:
Pacific Ocean

Country:
United States of America

Language:
English

Currency:
US Dollar

The Good . . .
- Malibu
- Point breaks
- Highway 101 (Pacific Coast Highway)

And the Bad . . .
- Malibu
- Parking
- Crowds

Los Angeles is an important location in surfing's history and culture. George Freeth, sometimes called the state's first surfer, demonstrated the sport near Redondo and Venice beaches in 1907. Many surfing firsts happened here, too, including the introduction of surfboard and surf-inspired soft-goods manufacturing; the filming and showing of the first surf movie; the first surf shop; and some of the first wetsuits to be designed for surfers. The evolution of modern surfboards started in L.A. with Tom Blake's first moves toward lighter surfboards, a trend furthered by innovations on the part of local luminaries such as Bob Simmons, Joe Quigg, and Dave Sweet.

Summertime provides the most surf excitement in L.A.'s northern half. Southern hemisphere swells spark reefs and point breaks at places such as Leo Carrillo, Point Dume, Malibu, Topanga Point, and Sunset, often

creating long, peeling right-hand rides fit for any type of board or surfer. These spots normally offer waves from two to four feet high between April and October, with occasional overhead lines when hefty waves arrive.

The most famous spot in the county, Malibu, has both good and bad qualities. Malibu's perfect point-break setup turns southerly walls into ruler-edge rides that can extend for hundreds of yards. On the flip side, the crowds that flock here all but prevent a person from catching a wave alone. Getting snaked here is the norm; some would say it is a requirement.

The southern half of the "City of Angels" holds more surfing opportunities in winter, between October and February. Beach breaks are most common here, with El Porto, Manhattan, Hermosa, and Redondo working best when broken-up wind swells create peaky, hollow conditions. The anomaly is Palos Verdes, an extremely localized run of reef breaks set below craggy cliffs. This holds the heavy stuff and really ignites at places like Indicator, Lunada Bay, Folos, Wally's, and B. A. Point. For the most part, though, if you do not live in PV you will not surf in PV. In fact, you might not even make it down the trail, as localism can prevail.

Below Local Sean Tully slips his longboard into the sweet spot of a glassy peeler in the northernmost reaches of Los Angeles County on a backlit, Santa Ana afternoon.

Surf San Diego

Location:
Pacific Ocean
Country:
United States of America
Language:
English
Currency:
US Dollar

The Good...
- Variety of wave types
- Wide swell windows
- Perfect climate

And the Bad...
- Crowds
- Pollution
- Occasional great white shark attacks

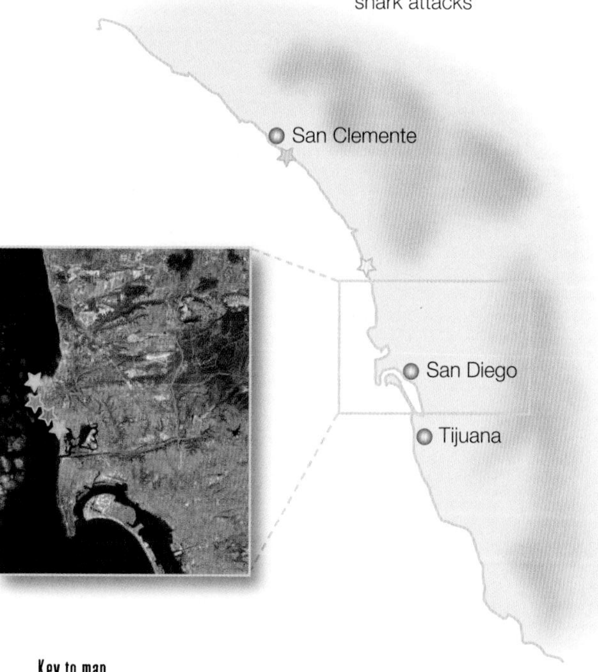

Key to map
- Trestles
- Black's Beach
- Little Point
- Simmons
- Windansea
- Big Rock

San Diego

Trestles, Black's Beach, Big Rock

San Diego County–the seventy-plus-mile range stretching from Trestles, just below the Orange County line, to the Tijuana Sloughs, near the Mexican border–receives swells year round, boasts the full gamut of wave types, has a pristine climate, and, in short, offers something for every surfer.

Surfing in San Diego started more than a century ago, when George Freeth spent considerable time in the mid-city beach towns teaching water-rescue techniques, coaching swimmers, and, of course, surfing. In the hundred years since, San Diego has been a home to countless famous surfers and surfboard shapers, has

hosted the 1966 and 1972 World Contests, and was California's first big-wave destination. It has also served as a testing ground for some of the sport's biggest equipment advancements, including the hard downrail, or tucked-under edge, surfboard designs by Anthony "Bunker" Spreckels and Michael Hynson, and Steve Lis's swallowtail keel fish.

At the extreme north end of San Diego County, often assumed to be located in Orange County, is Trestles, home to the only Association of Surfing Professionals (ASP) sanctioned contest in North America. Trestles is made up of two main spots–Lower Trestles and Upper Trestles–but Lower Trestles is the star of the show. With its unique setup–a flawless, point-style right and a shorter, wedging left, both beginning with perfect ramp walls off an A-frame peak–Lowers is world renowned, and for good reason.

The short, provincial stretch of La Jolla reefs is one of the best runs in the country, with Big Rock, Windansea, Simmons, and Little Point all close to each other. Big Rock, in particular, also known as Lobster Lounge, is a shallow-water, barreling left-hander. Its critical takeoff zone, located in front of a dry reef, wakes up with sizeable southern hemi swells.

Black's Beach is found at the foot of sheer, crumbly cliffs, favored by naked sunbathers and a packed house of surfers willing to hike down one of the steep trails. Black's is one of the world's finest beach breaks, highlighted by South Peak, an immaculate left-hand barrel that breaks from two to twenty feet.

Left San Diegan Sean Mattison rips through a full-rail turn on his swallowtail quad, somewhere in North County.

Right To the victor belong the spoils. An unknown rider drops into a South Peak left at Black's Beach.

Modern surfboard designs

The development of the surfboard—the one essential piece of surfing equipment—has been one of repeated trial-and-error in the quest to create faster, lighter, more maneuverable boards. The surfboard has evolved from the ancient, solid wood boards made from a single koa and wiliwili tree to the myriad of modern surfboards available today. Shaping machines now use computer programs to cut surfboards from space-age materials, and surfboards exist for every kind of wave, experience level, body type, gender, and age, and even for certain physical disabilities.

There are now shortboards, longboards, mid-length boards, slender boards, wide boards, thin boards, thick boards, foam boards, fiberglass boards, epoxy boards, and wood boards. Boards can come with wings, phasers, soft rails, hard-edged rails, knifey rails, pointed noses, or round noses; with one to five fins, or no fins at all. You can choose custom boards, built by hand, or generic boards pulled from the surf shop racks. The choice can be a bit overwhelming, but is really quite straightforward.

WHICH SURFBOARD IS FOR YOU?

First, what kind of surfer are you, and what kind of surfer are you aspiring to be? If you are a middle-aged beginner interested only in riding mellow waves on weekends, a mid-length board or longboard might best suit your need. If you are a young, intermediate surfer hell-bent on charging challenging waves and making the professional ranks, a refined shortboard or semi-gun will be essential as you prepare for your first foray to the North Shore.

As a general rule, though, learning to stand up on a surfboard lends itself to longboards, mid-lengths, or beefy shortboards. Remember that the longer, wider, and thicker a board is, the more stable it will be.

The surfboard you choose will depend on the surf you're planning to ride. If it is small, grab the longboard; if hollow and getting big, grab the semi-gun. With mediocre waves, try a fish or a retro board to boost the fun factor. You may need only two boards—a shortboard and a longboard—but owning more than three boards is fairly standard these days.

RETRO SINGLE FIN
Size: 7' to 8'
Fin setup: Single fin

SHORTBOARD
Size: 6' to 7'
Fin setup: Thruster

FISH
Size: 5'6" to 6'6"
Fin setup: Twin keels

SWALLOWTAIL QUAD
Size: 5'8" to 7'
Fin setup: Quad

HIGH PERFORMANCE LONGBOARD
Size: 8'6" to 10'
Fin setup: Center fin box plus side biters (a.k.a. "2+1")

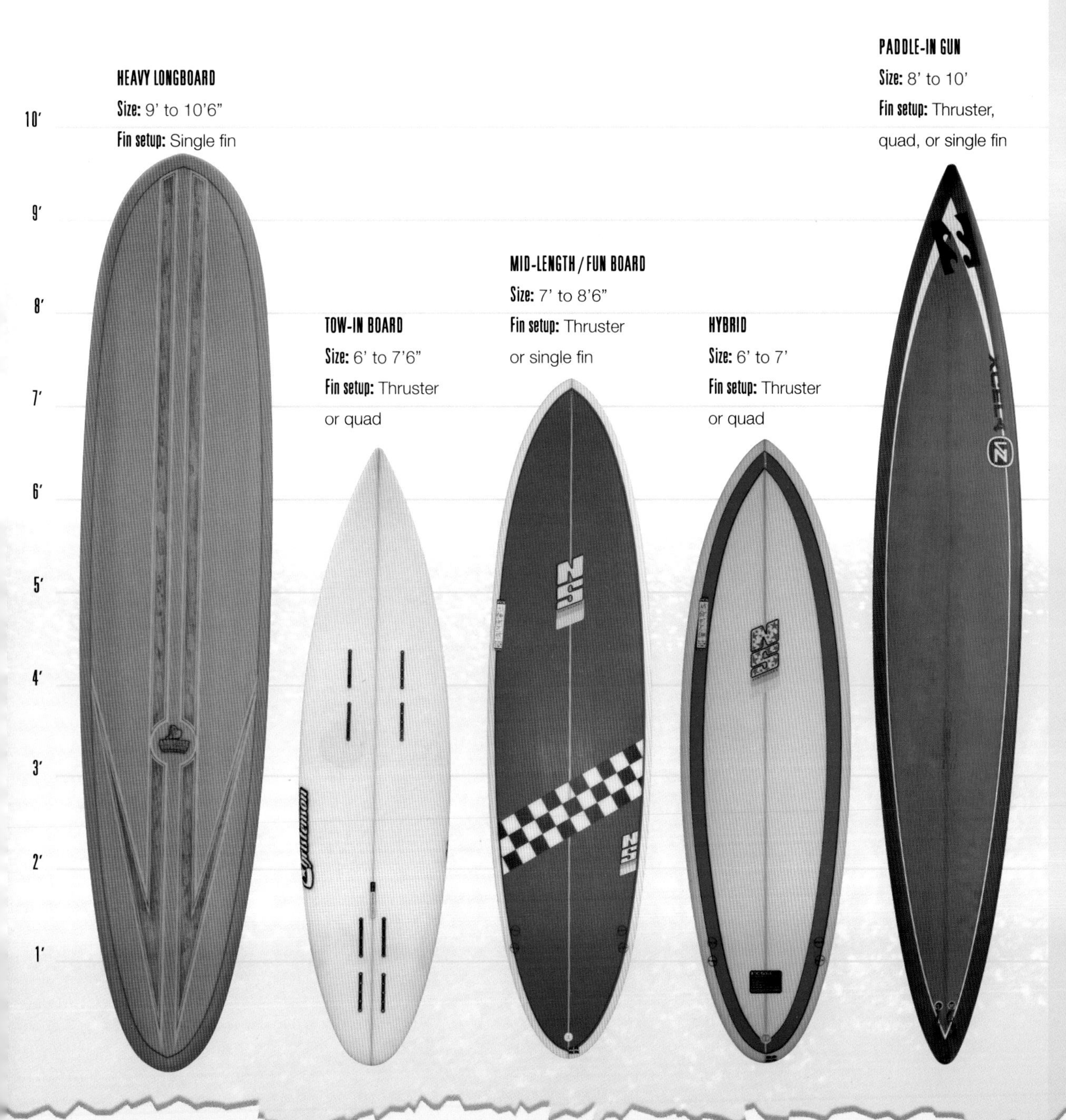

RIDING THE WAVES

Next, think about the kind of waves your board will be used on regularly. Will you ride sloping, long, California point breaks, hollow beach breaks like La Gravière, intense Indonesian reef breaks, outer-island big waves, or some combination thereof? You may want a single surfboard that can perform in every arena, but most modern shapes are designed with specific conditions in mind. Traditional longboards, or logs, all species of fish, mid-lengths, hybrids, and retro boards, usually with softer rails, are weapons of choice when it comes to surfing a point like Malibu. This is mainly because their width, flat rocker, and modest bottom concaves can plane across slow sections and create speed quickly.

Tackling steep sandbar and reef tubes requires something cleaner—like a thruster-style shortboard or semi-gun with more rocker, deeper concaves, and thinner rails with more bottom edge. This can quickly harness the wave's energy and allow you to maintain a higher line on the face. Paddling for giant waves can only be done with a full, narrow, pintail gun, sometimes called an elephant gun. The pintail gun will allow you to gather the paddle speed necessary to catch and drop in to a behemoth wave and outrun the menacing whitewater. Another point to consider is your desired surfing style. Do you want to surf with speed, style, power, and grace? Perhaps you want to surf in a high-performance manner, cruise with traditional flair, hang ten, hit the lip, trim, carve roundhouse cutbacks, or boost aerials. If you want to nose ride like Joel Tudor, then a heavy, single-fin log is for you; if you want to get beyond vertical and blow people's minds like Kelly Slater, then you need a thruster shortboard. If you want to do both, you will need at least two surfboards. Savvy surfers have come to realize that owning a quiver of boards is the best approach for having fun on a varied and ever-changing range of wave types.

Baja California

Cuatro Casas, Seven Sisters, Razors, Scorpion Bay

Surf Baja California

Location:
Pacific Ocean

Country:
Mexico

Language:
Spanish

Currency:
Peso

The Good . . .
- World-class waves
- Adventure

And the Bad . . .
- Difficult access
- Bandits
- Scorpions
- Crowds
- Corrupt officials

Key to map
- Cuatro Casas
- Punta Baja
- Seven Sisters
- Razors
- Scorpion Bay

Ensenada
BAJA NORTE
Gulf of California
BAJA SUR
Bahia San Juanico

Baja California, Mexico, has long been luring surfers from California and beyond. Those in search of classic point-break waves will find their navigational skills tested here. With no direct airport service and no beachside resorts to offer respite from the arid climate and rugged terrain, Baja's central coast remains mostly as it has for decades–rough and untouched.

Adventurous surfers seeking solace and uncrowded point surf have been exploring this stretch of Baja since the 1960s, on long and often dangerous road trips. The 1973 completion of the paved, two-lane Trans-Baja California Highway made north-south travels a bit easier, although no more safe. Reaching the Pacific remains a dusty and time-consuming affair, involving an unmarked, confusing tangle of dirt tracks, without any emergency services or gas stations around.

But for all the planning, packing, and driving required, there is treasure at the end of the trip. Some favorite stops, less than ten hours south of Tijuana, include Cuatro Casas, Punta Baja, and the Seven Sisters series of hard-to-find points. And Baja Sur (Baja South), farther down the road, is where the real gold zone can be found, especially from April through October, when south swells dominate the seascape.

Punta Abreojos, which translates to "Point Open Eyes," is a quaint fishing village at the end of a jarring road. A few waves exist here, like the fickle but fun town point and the hollow, shallow reef of Razors. Breaking barely above razor-clam-covered slabs, waves at Razors dare you to enter the lineup with the promise of perfectly round, right-hand tube rides. Be warned: the spot is named for the sharpness of those razor clams.

Above An azure ocean, a slight breeze, a palm-frond palapa, and a handmade hammock equal relaxation Mexican-style.

One of Baja's best lineups, though, resides at the end of a grueling drive. Some twenty-plus hours south of the United States border, and hidden behind a rut-covered road, sits Scorpion Bay, at the rim of the Bahia San Juanico. Scorps is an amazing stretch of point-break sections along a large point that can link up to form epic rides; such rides offer fast, flawlessly foiled, machinelike rights that spin from cove to cove. But such a ride is rare: Scorps, more often than not, separates into a handful of lineups, thus managing the usually thick crowd of campers.

Pure speed captured in a frozen frame: California's Jimmy Gamboa drives a classic fish design across a long point break somewhere in Baja California.

Cabo, Baja California

Cerritos, Zippers, Shipwrecks, Nine Palms

Above The warm Pacific Ocean laps an all-but undisturbed stretch of sandy beach in Cabo San Lucas.

The southern tip of Mexico's Baja California peninsula—from the eclectic town of Todos Santos to the touristy port of Cabo San Lucas and the quiet streets of San Jose del Cabo, and around to the barren East Cape reaches—has been a haunt since the 1950s for fishermen on a quest for the big catch and for surfers searching for a warm-water escape. A dry, desert region replete with cacti and lunar landscapes, Cabo's pleasant climate and wide range of accommodations—from dirt camping to wallet-slimming hotel spreads—attract hundreds of thousands of visitors during all but the hottest summer months, August through September, when temperatures are downright scorching.

Cabo is a short plane ride or two-day drive from Southern California, and it offers a variety of wave setups throughout the two swell seasons. Near Todos Santos, about an hour's drive northwest of Cabo, proper, hefty reefs, beaches, and points like Palm Beach, San Pedrito, Pescadero, and Cerritos offer the region's winter waves from November to March. Around the party town of Cabo San Lucas are the most crowded summer waves. Two of the busiest breaks, Monuments and Zippers, offer some of the best lefts and rights, respectively, from the port to the colonial town of San Jose del Cabo.

Heading northeast from San Jose, though, a stellar run of right-hand point breaks along the East Cape of the Sea of Cortez become wave wonderlands when strong weather systems or frighteningly close hurricanes push southerly swells into the gulf. Long, classic points, such as Shipwrecks, Nine Palms, Boca de Tule, and Punta Perfecta regularly draw those with maps marked with dirt roads and keen eyes for weather charts.

Key to map

- Pescadero
- Cerritos
- Monuments
- Zippers
- Shipwrecks
- Nine Palms
- Punta Perfecta
- Boca de Tule

Surf Cabo

Location:
Pacific Ocean

Country:
Mexico

Language:
Spanish

Currency:
Peso

The Good . . .
- Warm water
- Several wave zones
- Nearby nightlife

And the Bad . . .
- Hot and dry
- Crowded
- Hurricanes

Right An early season south swell awakens Zippers with just a few locals on hand to enjoy the surf.

Central Mexico

La Islita, La Ticla, Rio Nexpa, Pascuales

Surf Central Mexico

Location:
Pacific Ocean
Country:
Mexico
Language:
Spanish
Currency:
Peso

The Good . . .
- Tropical weather
- Warm water
- Range of waves

And the Bad . . .
- Insects
- Sharks
- Theft

Key to map
- Stoner's Point
- La Islita
- Pascuales
- La Ticla
- Guagua
- Rio Nexpa

San Blas
Guadalajara
Colima
Mexico City
Acapulco

Mainland Mexico has more than 2,000 miles (2,300 km) of coast fronting the Pacific Ocean and is open to both northern and southern hemisphere swells, plus waves created by seasonal tropical storms and hurricanes. Home to what many consider to be the world's best beach break, the world's longest right, and a great fetch of shoreline stacked to the brim with waves, "Mainland Mex" remains one of the planet's most popular surf destinations, more than fifty years after it was first explored by the surfer-filmmaker team of Greg Noll and Bud Browne.

Central Mexico's coastal region, stretching from the states of Nayarit to Michoacan, is blessed with a tropical climate and scenery, complete with banana, papaya, and mango trees and soaring, mountainous backdrops. This part of Mexico is also blessed with a lot of fun surf.

In Nayarit, the golden breaks are at Mantanchen Bay, near the town of San Blas. Stoner's Point, named after famous surf photographer Ron Stoner, is a classic point break with somewhat difficult access that can offer peeling right-handers for over a mile. Just south, though, La Islita–listed in *Guinness World Records* as having the

Below Las Islita, at Mantanchen Bay, is recognized as the world's longest surfable wave, capable of exhilarating rides of more than a mile.

longest right on Earth—can wrap waves around the point's rock outcroppings and line up easy walls and a few barrel sections for more than one-quarter of a mile with large south swells.

Colima and Michoacan have much heavier surf than Nayarit does, and it hits these states' beaches throughout the year. In Michoacan, a run of excellent river mouth waves lines the coast, the best being La Ticla, Guagua, and Rio Nexpa—all of which sport very hollow tubes and generally better lefts during south swell season. Pascuales, in Colima, however, is the number one peak in Central Mexico. A fun wave when it is small- to medium-sized, Pascuales really rises to the occasion when things get serious, producing gaping, powerful, left and right tubes that, for all except the most-skilled surfers, are sometimes better experienced from a shady palapa on the beach.

Above An out-of-the-tube view at Pascuales shows Californian pro Dane Reynolds setting up for the next barrel section.

Morning light over Puerto Escondido leads the way for Jaime Sterling on a gaping lefthander at Zicatela Beach.

Southern Mexico

Zicatela Beach, La Punta, secret spots

To surfers, the state of Oaxaca, Mexico, is famous for one thing–the massive, vicious sandbar barrels at Zicatela Beach in Puerto Escondido. Commonly known as "Puerto," the beach break was first attempted by traveling surfers toting heavy longboards in 1959, but it didn't become popular until the 1970s, when surfboards became much smaller and their shape became more refined, allowing them to handle top-to-bottom tubes such as those found here. More recently, the areas southeast of Puerto, toward Salina Cruz, have made headlines with an array of secret spots that can be tough to find but well worth the effort.

The once-quiet fishing village of Puerto Escondido is now a busy little town, which caters to a slew of international surfers eager to try their luck in the savage waves of Zicatela and indulge in some carousing and eating in between sessions. Come dawn, if the winds are calm, the thunder of a giant swell calls to visitors and the crew of talented locals hoping to slide into speeding, round tubes with an open exit door. Puerto gets very good indeed when a peaky, manageable, three- to six-foot swell rolls to town; however, when it gets close to ten feet the fierce surf easily separates the experts from the posers. And when it goes off the chain, look out! Puerto's waves can reach more than twenty feet (6 m) a few times a year, thanks to the deep-water trench offshore, creating double red-flag conditions that are dangerous even for professionals.

If giant death barrels are not your cup of tea, though, La Punta, a short bus ride from Zicatela, offers fun lefts; also, a stretch of excellent seasonal right-hand points and reefs is situated between Huatalco and Salina Cruz. Relatively new to the global surf map, this region is raw, windy, and wild, hidden behind confusing dirt tracks. But, armed with a four-wheel drive vehicle and some local knowledge, you may find it to be a serious score.

Surf Southern Mexico

Location:
Gulf of Tehuantepec, Pacific Ocean

Country:
Mexico

Language:
Spanish

Currency:
Peso

The Good . . .
- World-class waves
- Cheap
- Consistent wave quality

And the Bad . . .
- Very hot temperatures
- Crowds
- Bandits

Key to map
- Zicatela Beach
- La Punta

Oaxaca
Salina Cruz
Puerto Escondido
Huatulco

Left Soaking up the glow of the Pacific from a sandy edge in mainland Mexico.

Long Island, New York

Long Beach, Ditch Plains, Montauk

A mention of New York usually brings to mind images of Manhattan skyscrapers, traffic congestion, subways, and crowds of busy urbanites. Surfing in New York State, however, and especially on Long Island, is a world apart from the big-city scene.

Long Island projects into the Atlantic at a northeast angle, which opens the south-facing shoreline to hurricane swell as well as to east and southeast wind swell. However, the severe coastal curve and shadows cast by New England and Nova Scotia above restrict the amount of winter waves filtering in.

The break closest to Manhattan is Rockaway Beach, the only spot accessible via city subway, but the waves are not usually that great, the place is crowded, and the spot is mainly an easy place to escape from the city's day-to-day grind. Rockaway was the site of the historic 1912 surfing demonstration by surf icon and gold-medal swimmer Duke Kahanamoku, who stopped in New York on his way to Sweden for the Olympic Games.

On Long Island, though, both the topography and attitudes shift at spots such as Long Beach, Jones Beach, Robert Moses, and Fire Island, all of which lie within national park boundaries. A great deal of the peninsula, 130 miles (210 km) long, exists as it has for centuries due to federal protective measures as well as private ownership of some coastal stretches. Clean, sometimes powerful, beach breaks are the norm across most of Long Island, and jetties and groins at breaks such as Long Beach, Cupsogue, and Flies help to create desirable form.

Almost the only real reef and point setups are in and around Montauk, at the end of Long Island, a frustrating, three-hour drive from Manhattan. For the goofyfoot crew, few lefts are found here, but popular, longboard-friendly waves at Ditch Plains make this Montauk's best-known spot. Montauk has several high-quality waves that break above rock and sand bottom, including North Bar, Montauk Lighthouse, and Turtle Cove, a point-break setup at the tip of Long Island that holds bigger swells and can be very good, and very cold.

Surf Long Island

Location:
Atlantic Ocean

Country:
United States of America

Language:
English

Currency:
US Dollar

The Good . . .
- Empty stretches of beach breaks
- Dearth of serious surfers

And the Bad . . .
- Shortage of parking
- Crowds
- Bitterly cold winter water temperatures

Above Three friends stroll to the high-tide line at Long Beach, stoked to see empty, peaky perfection, and offshore conditions at their home break.

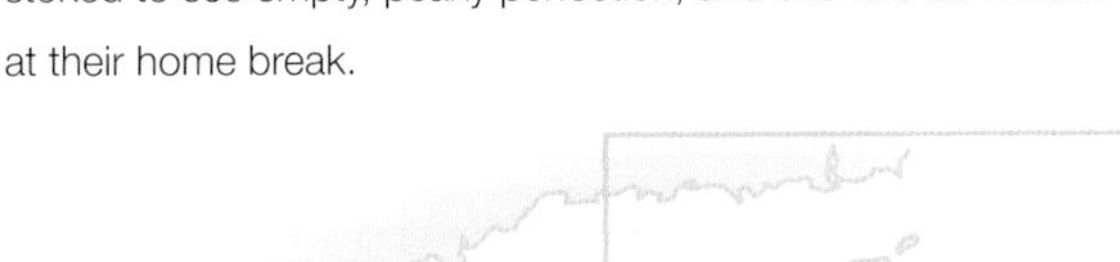

Key to map
- Long Beach
- Jones Beach
- Robert Moses
- Fire Island
- Cupsogue
- Ditch Plains
- Montauk
- Turtle Cove
- Lighthouse

Winters are cold in New York, but that doesn't stop the hardcore locals from getting in the water when good conditions present themselves—here, Pete McConnell, in mid-February slash.

North Carolina

Hatteras Lighthouse, Kitty Hawk Pier, Nags Head Pier

OUTER BANKS

Cape Hatteras

Key to map
- Kitty Hawk
- Nags Head
- Jeannette's
- Rodanthe
- Avon
- Lighthouse

An arcing strip of sandy islands, ninety miles (145 km) long, that forms a barrier beyond much of North Carolina's grassy coastline, the Outer Banks provide mile upon mile of good beach-break possibilities. Many of the popular spots, such as Kitty Hawk, Nags Head, Jeannette's, Rodanthe, and Avon, are named for the fishing piers they break near and around, but the biggest bonus of the Banks has to be the stretches of empty peaks that can be attained using a sturdy four-wheel-drive vehicle and a little perseverance.

The sandbars and water temperatures across the entire Outer Banks are constantly changing, thanks to the oceanic currents and unstable weather created at this convergence of the Labrador Current and Gulf Stream. Keep one eye on the horizon and query knowledgeable locals about the conditions and you can be richly rewarded: though unpredictable, the less-traveled path here can lead to unspoiled treasure.

Usually best between August and May, northeast swells provide the mainstay of fall and winter action and are given further boosts with hurricane-generated swells early in the season. Wave heights normally go from flat to six feet (2 m) across the Banks, with hefty hurricanes occasionally maxing out spots with ten- to twelve-foot surf. The waves formed along these fingers can get peaky, hollow, and punchy, but they can also disappear as fast as the warm water and sand do.

Cape Hatteras, also known as "Lighthouse," can be found in front of the tallest lighthouse in the United States, outside of Buxton–unmissable with its "barber pole" striped paint-job. This spot was first surfed in the early 1930s and is one of the best, and most popular, spots in North Carolina, drawing in swell and crowds from all directions. The shifting sand here creates everything from round, left, and right barrels to soft, mushy rollers. Lighthouse is also quite consistent, offering at least something to ride much of the year.

Surf North Carolina

Location:
Atlantic Ocean

Country:
United States of America

Language:
English

Currency:
US Dollar

The Good . . .
- High-grade waves
- Empty stretches of beach breaks
- Wildlife
- Hurricane swells

And the Bad . . .
- Summer crowds
- Surly fishermen
- Sharks
- Cold water temperature in winter

Right Outer Banks's Noah Snyder drives through a dramatically draining, October barrel at Rodanthe.

Below Clouds float in over the beach dunes and mixed-up sandbar surf on a summer day at the Outer Banks.

Riding on the Shoulders of Giants

"Surfing on a wave is a phenomenal conjunction of forces; the mathematics of it are profoundly complex."

—Drew Kampion, from *Stoked! A History of Surf Culture*

Mavericks Shifts Big-Wave Focus

During most of surfing's history, Hawaii was thought to be the home of the only legitimate big waves, those over twenty feet (6 m) tall, but the 1990s signaled the start of a global search for big waves. The first of these monsters, now known as Mavericks, was tackled in the sleepy California town of Half Moon Bay.

Local surfer Jeff Clark had quietly ridden the wave alone for fifteen years. "It was a great confidence boost for me to have gone where no one had gone before," Clark later told Maverickssurf.com, "and to ride waves that were more powerful than anything that I had ever imagined." Few people listened to his tales of the heavy surf breaking just off Pillar Point until a 1992 *Surfer* magazine article officially kicked the cat out of the bag, making Mavericks the big-wave mecca of the continental United States. "It's the biggest, baddest paddle-in spot in the world," continued Clark. "When it comes to who's paddling into the biggest waves on this planet, it's the guys that surf here."

Mavericks has been pitching out lips like this for longer than most can fathom, but the popular big-wave venue has only been ridden by brave surfers for the past few decades.

Killer waves

One hundred miles (160 km) off the coast of San Diego, Cortes Banks—particularly a peaking segment of the massive, undersea mountain range—is a red-zone hazard for fishermen and seafarers. A few surfers, though, recognized the big-wave potential of Cortes in the 1960s, and scouting missions in the 1990s confirmed it.

In 2001, Billabong Odyssey's "Project Neptune" expedition descended in the dark of night, with two boats of surfers, photographers, video shooters, and personal watercraft, all joined at dawn by a low-altitude airplane. During the morning hours, two respected tow-in teams rode Cortes' gigantic, glassy swells. The experiment climaxed when Mike Parsons caught a beast that measured roughly 65 feet (20 m), officially the biggest wave ever ridden off North America and one of the biggest ridden on Earth. If riding a 100-foot (30 m) wave is possible, this is where it could happen.

South of the border is another legendary offshore wave. Killers—at Isla de Todos Santos, off Ensenada, Mexico—has lured surfers for decades. Thanks to an underwater canyon at the northwestern edge of the island, north swells funnel in and can near 40 feet (12 m). One of the globe's best paddle-in big waves and, now, a popular tow-in spot, Killers has helped pros like Taylor Knox and Brad Gerlach win biggest-wave-of-the-year awards.

Below Killers, found at Isla de Todos Santos, off mainland Mexico, shows some very serious size.

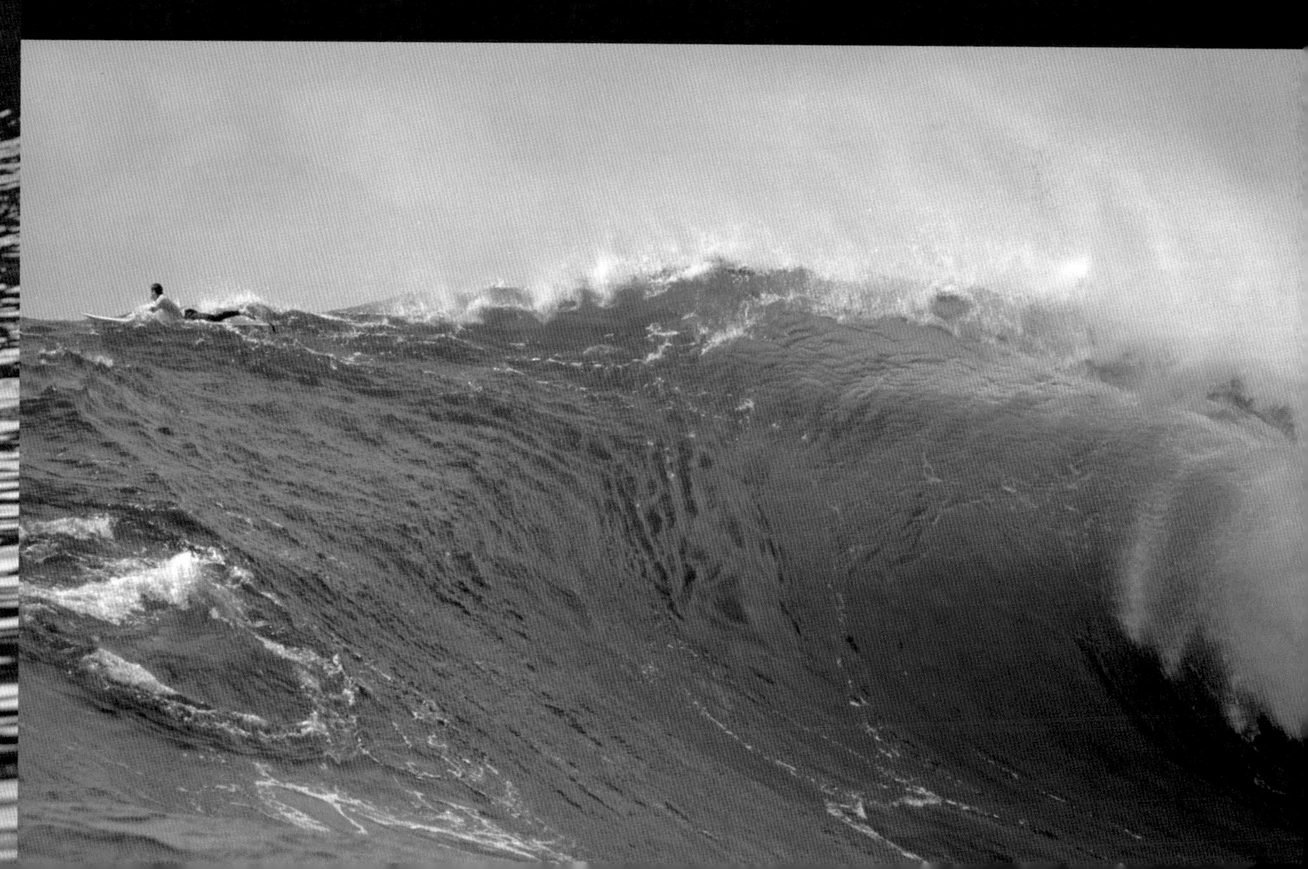

The Biggest Waves on North America's West Coast

- Nelscott Reef, Oregon
- Yeti, Oregon
- Potato Patch, California
- Mavericks, California
- Ghost Tree, California
- Tijuana Sloughs, California
- Cortes Banks, California
- Killers, Baja California, Mexico
- Zicatela Beach, Mexico

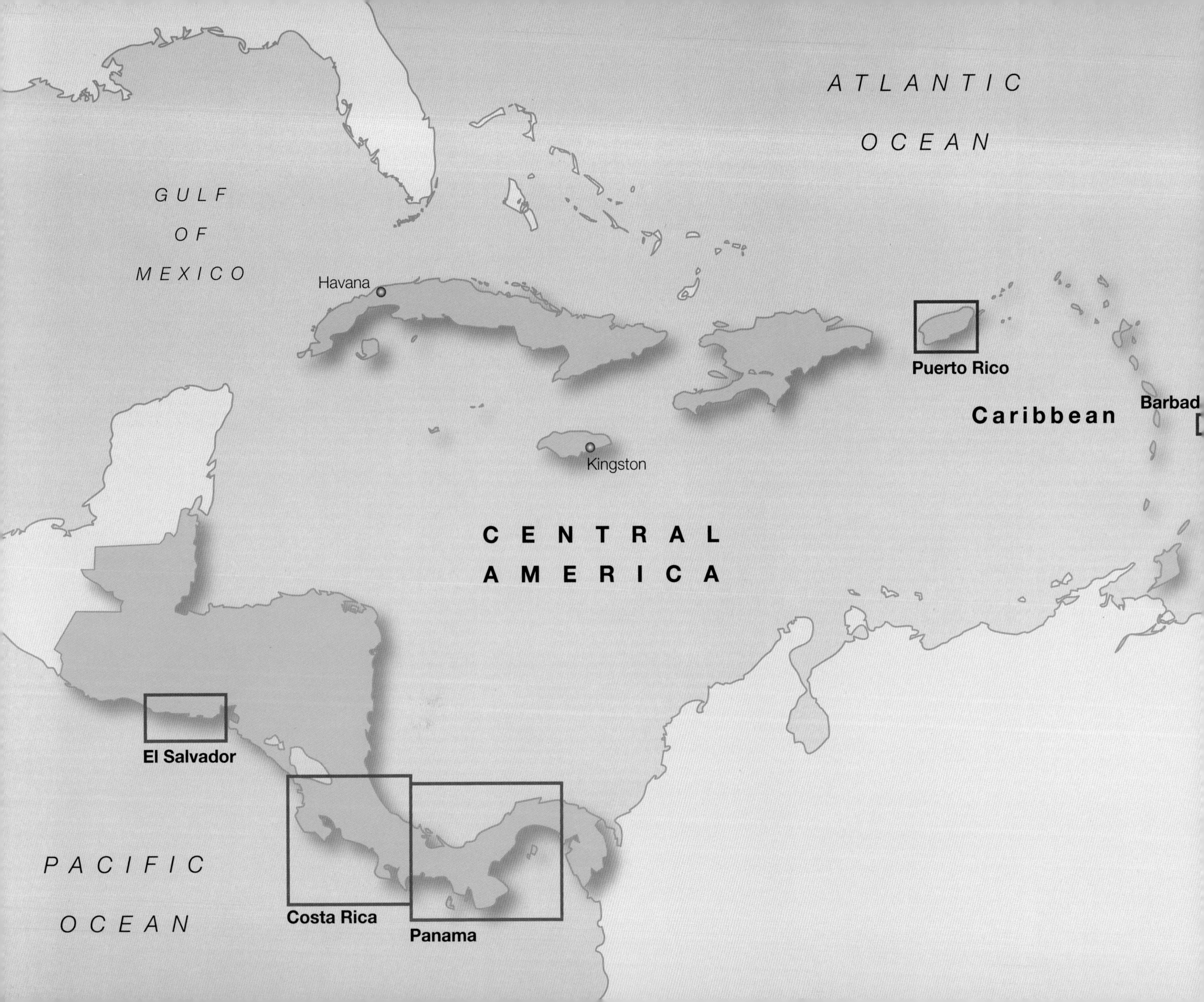
ATLANTIC
OCEAN
GULF
OF
MEXICO
Havana
Puerto Rico
Barbad
Caribbean
Kingston
CENTRAL
AMERICA
El Salvador
PACIFIC
OCEAN
Costa Rica
Panama

Central America / Caribbean

The disparate surf areas of Central America and the Caribbean have been a favorite haunt since pioneering surfers began foraying into the region in the 1940s. Cheap food and accommodation plus a familiar, yet simultaneously exotic, language and culture played a large part in the area's allure. But what drew wave prospectors to these beaches in their droves were the hundreds of miles of empty, unexplored surf. From Puerto Rico to Panama, some spectacular gems were unearthed.

These surfing pioneers went on extended road trips to deep inside jungles located in lawless territories. Nowadays, there's no need to tote a gun when visiting these shores. Nor is there any need to endure interminable journeys. Getting here, being here, and getting out of here is as hassle-free as any stateside vacation. While some countries, such as Nicaragua, El Salvador, and Panama, previously had a bad reputation, most of the internal strife, frightening political tensions, and military coups are now distant memories. The whole region is wide open for exploration. Notwithstanding, driving alone or at night is to be avoided, as roadside bandits operate in some areas. Rains can wash out roads during the wet season, so be wary of the weather. Tropical diseases and mosquitoes pose a threat to health, but can, in the main, be prevented and treated. When it comes to surfing, though, things are relatively safe. Shark attacks are rare, especially on the Pacific side, although crocodiles do occasionally cross paths with surfers. Also to be avoided are the polluted waters near rivermouths and town beaches.

While the climate is mainly tropical, there is variation between the drier winter months and the hot, rainy season. Inland or around the coast, the landscape is diverse and wondrous. This kaleidoscope of spectacular mountain scenery and waterfalls, warm, golden sands, and palm-fringed beaches, is bordered by the Pacific Ocean to the west and the Caribbean Sea to the east.

The entire region offers many venues for adventurous surfers to escape the day-to-day rat race and score some bodacious waves in a slower-paced, laid-back atmosphere. Armed with a smile, love for the locals, tolerance, respect, and a heap of good vibes, Central America is likely to provide a vacation and tides to remember for a lifetime.

El Salvador

El Zonte, Zunzal, Punta Roca

El Salvador has a limited fetch of Pacific-facing coastline, only about 150 miles (240 km) of it, but the small Central American country does a great deal with what it has. A tropical place with warm ocean temperatures and even warmer weather, El Salvador's shore is ideally angled to the south and, between April and October, produces high-quality rights, highlighted by a number of great point breaks.

Reports of the possibilities of El Salvador's right-hand waves began trickling into North America in the 1960s and '70s. Unfortunately, an ugly civil war ravaged the country in the 1980s, keeping all but the most thick-skinned–or foolhardy–surf travelers out. In the more than twenty years since, though, tourists and a local expatriate population have made their way to the country to ride its classic waves.

Many of the most popular spots are to be found around the town of La Libertad, with a host of others still hidden to the east and west behind almost impossible terrain that is accessible only by boat. El Zonte is a shallow right point, best surfed on a high tide in order to avoid the slew of boulders, but Zunzal, a consistent point break with several barrel sections, found west of town, collects the biggest crowds.

In the heart of La Libertad sits Punta Roca, El Salvador's claim to fame. One of the best rights in Central and South America, Punta Roca starts with a steep takeoff that tubes before wrapping into the bay. It lengthens into a speedy, down-the-line, high-performance wall with several other opportunities for barrels over the boiling boulders along the 250-yard (228 m) ride to the inside.

Key to map
- El Zonte
- Zunzal
- Punta Roca

Surf El Salvador

Location:
Pacific Ocean
Country:
El Salvador
Language:
Spanish
Currency:
Colones

The Good . . .
- Great righthand point breaks
- Cheap
- Empty lineup possibilities

And the Bad . . .
- Pollution
- Bandits
- Urchins

Right A local El Salvadorian surfer enjoys a swift, down-the-line right at Punta Roca while another appreciates the scene from the rocks.

Below Waterfalls in Juayua, deep within the country's rainforest interior.

Costa Rica

Ollie's Point, Witches Rock, Marbella, Matapalo, Pavones

Originally named the "Rich Coast" by Christopher Columbus, Costa Rica is one of those glorious locations that offer a variety of waves for surfers of every skill level, accommodations from cheap cabinas to luxury resorts, and a sense of safety in a strange land. Costa Rica has, in modern times, been the most peaceful and

Left Floridian Paul Reineke tucks into a hollow wall at one of the shapely beachbreaks outside Tamarindo.

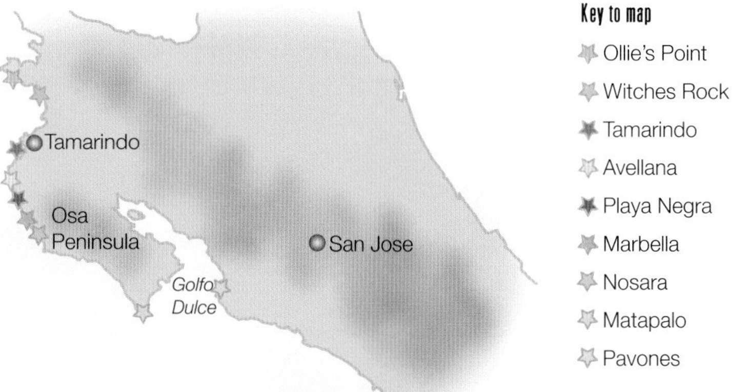

Key to map

- Ollie's Point
- Witches Rock
- Tamarindo
- Avellana
- Playa Negra
- Marbella
- Nosara
- Matapalo
- Pavones

Surf Costa Rica

Location:

Pacific Ocean

Country:

Costa Rica

Language:

Spanish

Currency:

Colones

The Good . . .

- Large variety of good waves
- Waves are consistent
- Friendly people
- Beautiful scenery

And the Bad . . .

- Snakes
- Insects
- Rip currents
- Crocodiles

Left Crossing rivers over sketchy wooden bridges in Costa Rica is par for the track.

At Pavones, gorgeous black sand beaches are just a short drive out of the point and around the corner.

stable country in Central America. The nation has avoided the internal unrest and economic issues that have plagued neighbors like Nicaragua, Panama, Honduras, and El Salvador, and it has been without a national military since 1949.

Although Costa Rica's tasty waves were initially ridden by American surfers during the 1960s, the untamed, tropical wilderness didn't really make much noise as a popular surfing stop until almost two decades later. The country quickly became known as a fantastic wave and vacation destination soon thereafter, though. Its friendly people, warm water and climate, cheap land, and easygoing vibe (that is, everywhere but in the capital city, San Jose) further enticed American and international expatriates in search of a slow-paced lifestyle and good surf to settle here.

Costa Rica is blessed with waves most of the year, receiving a hardy diet of south and southwest swells between April and November, and Arctic lines from the northwest between November and March. With surf heights generally ranging from two to six feet (0.6–2 m), and rarely reaching heights of eight to ten feet (2.5–3 m), Costa Rica is best known for the high-quality form of its surf rather than its frightening nature.

Far north, along the Pacific shore, the Guanacaste province is one of the country's most consistent areas, accepting year-round swells. Tamarindo is at its heart, and is the most tourist-oriented town around. A fun right at the river mouth and a handful of other crowded spots exist here, but most hard-core surf travelers either use Tamarindo as a base camp and party stop or avoid it altogether, focusing instead on the stellar run of beaches and reefs to the south, such as Avellana, Playa Negra, and Nosara. One of the lesser-surfed yet high-grade breaks nearby is Marbella, a sand- and reef-bottomed wave capable of very deep right and left tube rides.

Some surfers travel to the Guancaste for the specific task of riding one or both of the province's pair of classic northern spots, Ollie's Point and Witches Rock. Though often crowded with boats, Ollie's classic rights can get absolutely perfect, especially when sculpted by offshore winds. Witches Rock, just south of Ollie's, is a world-renowned, hollow, peeling beach break with several opportunities for in-and-out barrels aside its namesake, a massive, rocky chunk.

Golfo Dulce is located in the deep south, home to more than a dozen named breaks, including two epic points and countless others concealed behind near-impenetrable jungle. At the tip of the gulf's west shore sits Matapalo, a three-part point break that ignites into speedy, rock-bottomed, right-hand waves with a number of hollow sections on south or westerly swells. Tucked deeper inside the bay, on the east side, Pavones can be reached with a sturdy four-wheel-drive. Ironically, for an area so difficult to reach, the main wave gets incredibly crowded; luckily, Pavones happens to be one of the planet's longest left-hand points, and the quarter-mile rides and pulling currents do a good job of spreading out the pack. Pavones works best when solid swells fill the gulf, but when that happens a leg-burningly long fetch of high-performance walls over cobblestones can connect from the point, past the Esquina del Mar cabinas, and down to the beached fishing boats.

Below right British longboarder Jim Newitt hangs five across a perfect right during a golden, first-light session at the famed Ollie's Point.

Panama

Silverbacks, Morro Negrito, Santa Catalina, Rio Mar

The small country of Panama is a wave-riding paradise. With several regions of surfing possibilities, affordable accommodation, few tourists, and tropical water and weather, Panama satisfies the urge for good waves in a foreign atmosphere.

Waves enter Panama's swell window from a few directions and across two oceans, so surfing here can be done year-round. The Pacific side works best when south and southwest waves approach, from March into October; on the country's Caribbean coast, northeast and east swells keep it busy between November and March. Not known for its death-defying venues, Panama surfing does get big and contains a full list of fun setups: beach breaks, reefs, right and left points, river mouths, and plenty of barrier islands.

The northern, Caribbean side is covered with beautiful islands, including Colon, which is in the Bocas del Toro area. Bocas del Toro, like much of Panama, boasts an impressive résumé of wondrous water clarity and spicy reef breaks, including the dredged barrels at Dumps, long and hollow lefts at Paunch, and thick right tubes at Silverbacks.

The southwest coast, from Morro Negrito to Santa Catalina, is a dense concentration of jungle, reefs, and offshore islands. Many of the islands, especially Silva de Afuera, Coiba, and Cebaco, are blessed with good surf, so short boat trips are common here and throughout Panama. Swells in this region also pass the islands and hit the mainland at Morro Negrito and Santa Catalina. At Morro is a right-hand racetrack tube and, just south, Rivermouth deals endless lefts; Santa Catalina is home to a right point, making for consistent hot-dogging surf.

In and around Panama City, though, exists a fickle but very good stretch of reefs, river mouths, and point breaks. The south swell needs to be angled perfectly, and, when it is, at least twenty spots start cracking and the area becomes a land of wave possibility. A few names to remember here include La Zurda, Playa Malibu, Playa Serena, Punta Teta, Rinconsito, San Carlos, Punta Palmar, and Rio Mar.

Surf Panama

Location:
Pacific Ocean and Caribbean Sea

Country:
Panama

Language:
Spanish and English

Currency:
Balboa and US Dollar

The Good . . .

- Multiple wave regions
- Few crowds
- Wave variety
- Tropical climate

And the Bad . . .

- Difficult wave access
- Disease
- Shallow reefs
- Thieves

Below A powerful, hollow left goes unridden somewhere in the Bocas del Toro province.

Right Located off Panama's Caribbean coast, the turquoise maze of major islands, islets, and mangrove cays that make up Bocas del Toro is home to some excellent surf spots.

Puerto Rico

Gas Chambers, Crash Boat, Domes, Little Malibu, Tres Palmas

Surf Puerto Rico

Location:
Atlantic Ocean

Country:
Puerto Rico

Language:
English and Spanish

Currency:
US Dollar or Peso

The Good . . .
- World-class reef breaks
- Offshore winds

And the Bad . . .
- Sea urchins
- Competitive crowds
- Crime
- Polluted runoff

Key to map
- Motones
- Jobo's
- Surfer's Beach
- Gas Chambers
- Crash Boat
- Domes
- Maria's
- Tres Palmas
- Little Malibu

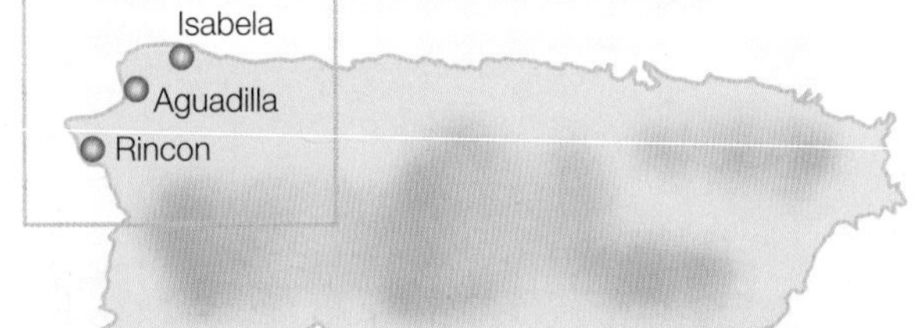

For many surfers based on the East Coast of the United States, Puerto Rico, found 1,000 miles (1,600 km) off Miami, Florida, is a place to escape the mainland routine beachbreaks and experience some welcome reefs and point breaks. Puerto Rico provides powerful, high-quality Caribbean Island surf refined by lava and coral. It offers the chance to tackle legitimate big waves, much like its West Coast island counterpart, Hawaii. And, furthering comparisons, Puerto Rico boasts tropical weather, warm ocean temperatures, exotic scenery, and an impressive cadre of homegrown surfers.

There are at least twenty high-grade surf spots on the northwestern corner of the island, between the towns of Isabela and Rincon. These are generally best from October into March, when low pressure systems drop down from the North Atlantic Ocean and slide onto a fruitful, coastal headland. This short stretch is the Atlantic's answer to Oahu's North Shore. Most of these breaks cater to experienced and expert wave riders when the surf is in the three- to six-foot (1–2 m) range, but beginner waves can be found, too, with a little driving to more sheltered areas.

Around Isabela, slightly less pressured spots, including Motones, Jobo's, and Surfer's Beach, can get very good. Closer to Aguadilla, famous but fickle reefs at Gas Chambers and Crash Boat will work to perfection and create round tubes with big or north-northwest swells, but on such a small island word gets out fast and lineups quickly get cramped when that happens. Domes, Maria's, Little Malibu, and a stretch of lesser-known reef breaks surround the point outside the town of Rincon, which is also where Tres Palmas is found.

The biggest wave on Puerto Rico, and certifiable with waves to twenty feet (6 m) or more, Tres Palmas is the Caribbean's answer to Sunset Beach or Waimea Bay. At reasonable size, Tres Palmas is the best wave on the island. But if you get to see Tres Palmas really doing its thing, grab a piña colada, sit back, and enjoy the sight.

Above Another method of transportation through the Caribbean: seaplane bliss.

Tres Palmas goes extra large thanks to a recent swell to remember, and American expatriate Dennis Ritch was in prime position to reap the sweet rewards.

Barbados

South Point, Tropicana, Duppies, Soup Bowls

The easternmost island in the West Indies, Barbados is blessed with fun, consistent surf, an immaculate climate, perfect ocean temperatures, a turquoise ocean, and a laid-back vibe. Though big waves are scarce on this island, which was once dubbed the "Island of the Bearded One," breakers up to six feet (2 m) occur on the north and west sides, most often between November and April. These are sent down from winter storms that move in from the North Atlantic Ocean. Regular trade winds create waves that keep Barbados's east coast working nearly year-round, with hurricane-generated swells helping to liven up the eastern and southern shores.

The variety of breaks on Barbados, from white-sand beaches to coral reefs and points, make the island a good fit for everyone from surfing families on vacation to bachelor wave-hunters with months to wait for optimum conditions. While surf is spotty on the south coast, it gets good at places like Silver Sands, Freights, and the solid left-hander of South Point, when hurricanes spin past. The island's west coast suffers from island blockage by Puerto Rico's Caribbean neighbors and, as a result, is the least consistent region. But, big north swells will awaken the west side's rare, exotic birds like Sandy Lane and Tropicana.

The northern edge of Barbados has high-risk, high-reward waves at spots such as North Point and Duppies, but this area requires a bit more of an adventurer's spirit and, again, good north swell. The most popular area of Barbados is found around the eastern town of Bathsheba. Home to Conset Point, Tent Bay, Parlors, and Soup Bowls, this area is open to thousands of miles of Atlantic action and lures pulses from a bevy of directions. Soup Bowls, specifically, is the island's best and most consistent wave. Sometimes said to have rideable surf nearly every single day, the reef setup at Bowls bends swells into fast rights with a perfectly round tubing takeoff section, high-performance walls, and a tropical backdrop to rival any on Earth.

Above Coconut palms, white sands, and a tropical breeze welcome surfers to the south coast of Barbados—a tropical island idyll for sun worshippers and wave riders alike.

Right Australian professional Claire Bevilacqua rips a quick top turn during a small day session at Soup Bowls.

Surf Barbados

Location:
Atlantic Ocean and Caribbean Sea

Country:
Barbados

Language:
English

Currency:
Barbadian Dollar

The Good . . .
- Laid-back vibe
- Warm water
- Friendly people

And the Bad . . .
- Rip currents
- Urchins
- Wind

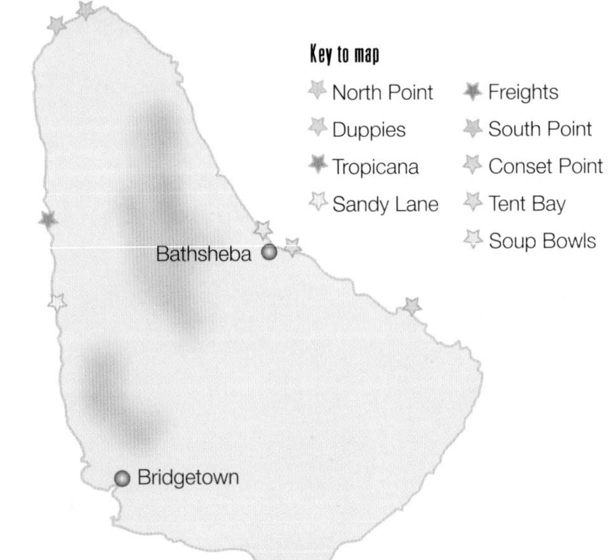

Surfmobiles

Surfers have always viewed their automobiles as primarily a way to drive themselves, their friends, and surfboards to the waves. Nearly any mechanically sound car, truck, or wagon does the job. It doesn't matter if the front seat is a folding chair, the fenders are dented, the paint is mismatched, or the dash is missing—if it runs and a board can be shoved inside or strapped onto the roof, then hop in! The most popular surfmobiles are sturdy, dependable, and spacious enough to carry stacks of boards, soggy and sandy trunks, towels, wetsuits, and gear at a moment's notice.

WEIRD AND WONDERFUL WAGONS

For many, the "woodie" station wagon is the iconic surfmobile. The idyllic image of a beachside woodie wagon, parked overlooking the waves, with vintage longboards sticking out the back window is a symbol of the surf counterculture. First manufactured by the Ford Motor Company in the 1930s and '40s as a way to reduce production costs by limiting the amount of steel in its automobiles, it was followed by a slew of woodie wagon models from most other American makers. Surfers in the 1950s and '60s took advantage of the wide availability of these used, inexpensive, often discarded rides. Not only was the woodie a substantial board and body courier, but it also provided a place to sleep on overnight trips.

Ironically, the cheap and sometimes beaten-up woodie station wagons of that short era had become much sought-after restoration projects by the end of the 1960s, and fixing them up is a trend that attracts serious motor-heads and car collectors around the world to this day, with some resurrected and "cherry" woodies selling for more than $100,000.

Top left The Volkswagen camper van, which, more than a half century after its first manufacture, is still the world's greatest surfmobile.
Top right The only question that has ever mattered when it comes to a surfmobile is, "How many surfboards can you fit in that thing?"
Below left The "woodie" station wagon—arguably the most iconic surfmobile of all time.
Below center No door? No problem! Just so long as it gets my surfboard to the beach, officer.
Below Right The new-era global surfmobile—the brute sports utility vehicle, or "SUV" for short.

In 1950, just as many woodies were being shelved by their manufacturers, Volkswagen launched its Type 2 line, or Transporters, which would become perhaps the most popular surfmobile of all time. Commonly referred to as the VW van, hippie bus, microbus, or Kombi, used Transporters could be purchased fairly inexpensively and were quickly established as the perfect surfmobiles. The van was spacious and offered several seating plans, window configurations, and options like tables, foldout beds, and kitchenettes in the camper editions. Plus, its rear engine was easy to reach and work on, with replacement parts affordable and readily available just about anywhere. Over the decades, surfers in Europe, Africa, Australia, North and South America, and beyond set up at local shores in style and comfort, and hit the road with the help of VW vans in search of off-the-beaten-path wave breaks. Early VW buses are still seen trekking to desolate beaches around the globe and new vans are still being produced more than fifty years on. And, as is the case with woodies, refurbishing classic Transporters is a serious hobby for many.

NEW-ERA SURFMOBILES

Downfalls of the VW vans were their limited ground clearance and difficulty driving in sand and across dirt or muddy roads. As the golden age of surf exploration went into full swing in the late 1960s and '70s, reaching the coast in places like Africa, Central and South America, and Australia required rugged four-wheel drives. The civilian answer to muscular military vehicles, popular mobiles of the era included Jeeps, especially the Willys Wagon, the International Harvester Scout, Ford Bronco, Toyota Land Cruiser FJ models, and the Land Rover. These longer-wheelbase, wagon-type autos set the stage for all Sports Utility Vehicles that followed, a genre that has stayed atop the surfmobiles' list into the present day.

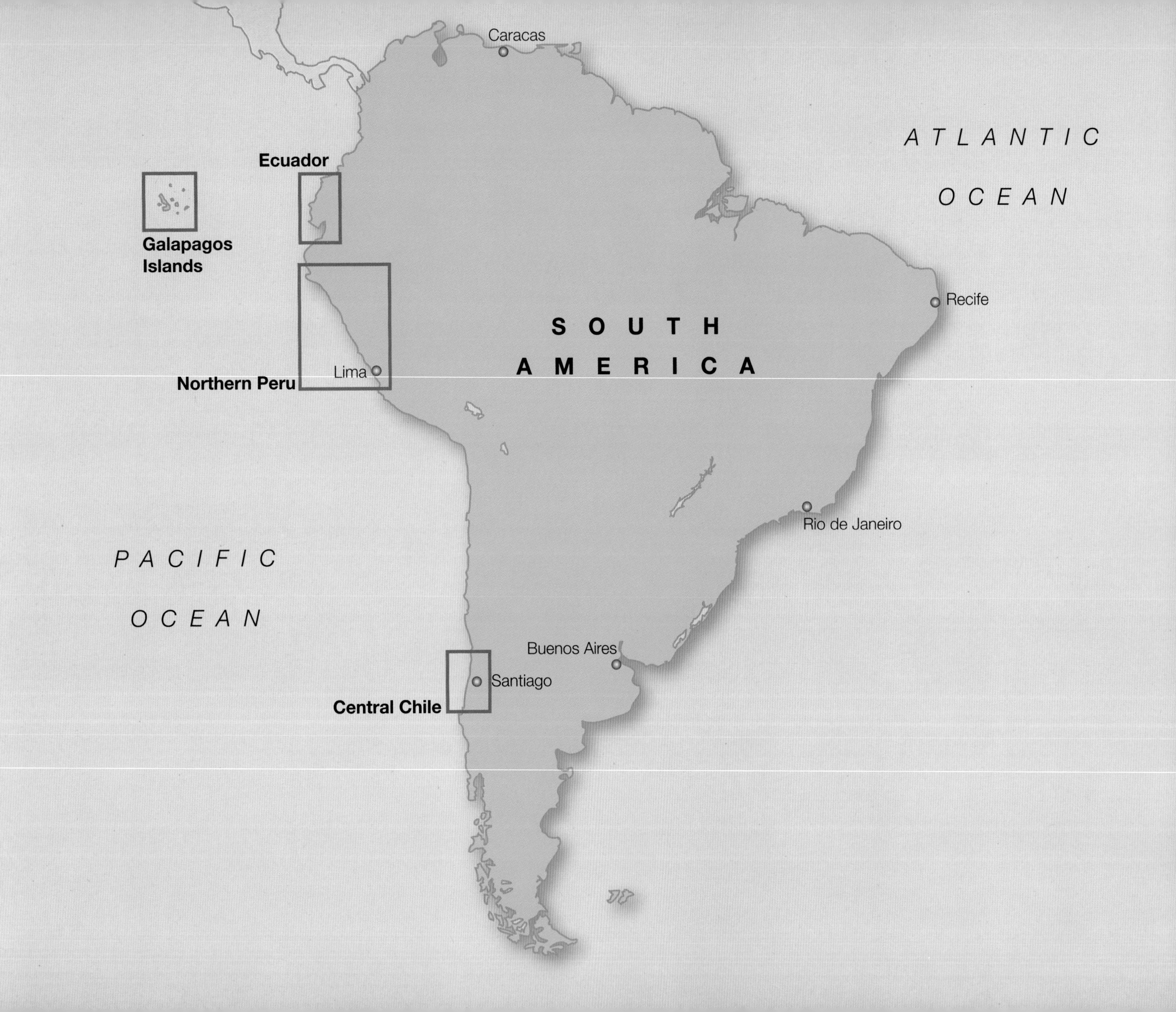
Caracas
ATLANTIC
OCEAN
Ecuador
Galapagos
Islands
Recife
SOUTH
AMERICA
Lima
Northern Peru
Rio de Janeiro
PACIFIC
OCEAN
Buenos Aires
Santiago
Central Chile

South America

This is a continent that receives swells from all angles, and is home to millions of surfers. South America can be surfed almost every day of the year, especially along its South Pacific shore, and its coast offers every type of wave imaginable. From wind-borne, beach-break mush to intense, world-class big waves formed from strong Antarctic systems, and even tidal bores in the Amazon river, this wonderfully wave-rich continent has something for everyone.

The continent has a variety of surfing histories, from ancient to more recent. In Peru, pre-Inca cultures such as the Chimu and Mochica left artifacts, mainly ceramics, detailing their close relationship with waves and tides. According to legend, the first people to practice an early form of surfing here were fishermen who rode into the ocean to harvest food. Later, at the turn of the twentieth century, a group of Lima surfers were riding "drawing boards" purely for fun outside the town of Barranco. By contrast, it seems that the first local surfer did not take to the ocean in Chile until around 1970.

This landmass is truly one of staggering environmental contrasts, home as it is to some of the densest, most undeveloped places in the world, such as the Amazon Basin, Patagonia, and the Andes mountain range, and also one of the most populous cities on the planet, São Paulo. It is home to Earth's largest river as well as its driest desert. Unfortunately, one thing these disparate regions share in common is a serious ocean pollution problem. Untreated sewage is dumped into rivers, and industrial waste is deposited by careless corporations that are all-too aware of the continent's weak environmental laws. Some of South America's beaches and bays are the dirtiest in the world.

The good news for surfers interested in riding the innumerable breaks in South America is that, with help from watchdog groups like Save The Waves, strides have been made toward enhanced effluent-treatment plants and more stringent laws. The problems are slowly improving. And, quite apart from this, much of South America's less populous southern half has clean ocean conditions, while Ecuador's Galapagos Islands form one of the most pristine, undisturbed natural areas in the world.

Ecuador

Mompiche, San Mateo, Montañita

Above The bow of a beached boat in Puerto Lopez.

Right Puerto Rican surfer Brian Toth gets loose on a lively one at San Lorenzo, north of Esmeraldas.

Ecuador may not be as big as its southern neighbors, Peru and Chile, but the Panama current means ocean temperatures are much warmer here, and the coast from the north to center has a large number of good breaks, spread between several positively great breaks. Straddling the equator, Ecuador gets blazing hot, making seasonal rain showers a more than welcome respite.

The country's unstable political situation and sketchy travel information kept Ecuador out of the surfing spotlight for decades after the sport was first practiced on its shore in the early 1960s; thankfully, though, the local military personnel do not harass surfers as much as they used to, and most of the violent crime has since been pushed into Quito and the territories of the extreme north bordering Colombia. Since the 1980s, traveling surfers and surf photographers have returned from Ecuador with tales of good waves and wondrous sessions, and the images to back up their stories.

More than thirty varied breaks, from points to reefs to beach breaks, exist between the towns of Esmeraldas and Playas, and consistent surf enters the region all year thanks to Ecuador's northwest and southwest swell windows. Three of the best are Mompiche, San Mateo, and Montañita. Mompiche is a dreamy left point that is hollow, very long, and set in an emerald ocean with beautiful surroundings. The little fishing village of San Mateo isn't much to look at, or smell, but there is a solid, left-hand, point-style wave there that is always worth checking. San Mateo is fickle but pays dividends when it's on. And then there is Montañita, a consistent, grinding right near San Jose. Montañita can hold waves past double overhead and is known for its heavy barrels.

Surf Ecuador

Location:
Pacific Ocean

Country:
Ecuador

Language:
Spanish and Quechua

Currency:
US Dollar

The Good . . .
- Warm water
- Wave variety
- Cheap

And the Bad . . .
- Disease
- Petty crime

Key to map
- Mompiche
- San Mateo
- Montañita

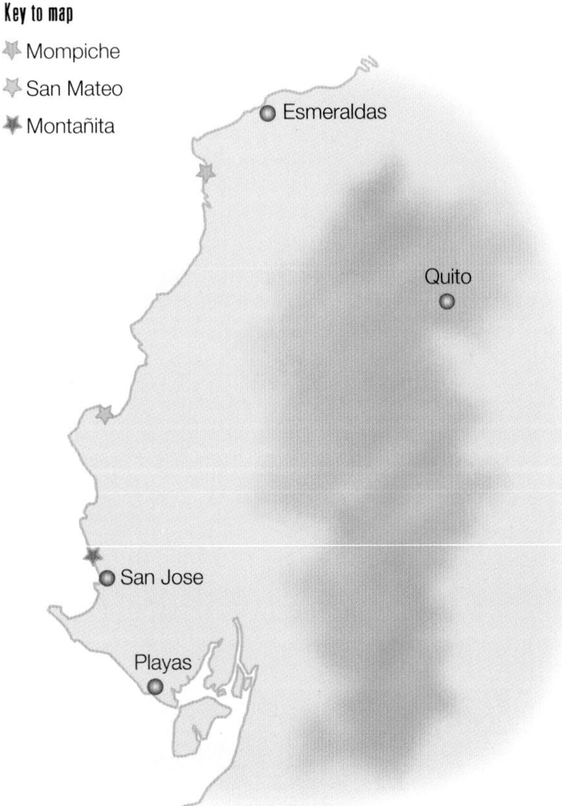

Galapagos Islands

Tongo Reef, Loberia, El Canyon, Carola

A World Heritage Site and massive marine refuge, the Galapagos Islands form one of the planet's natural wonders. Though the Galapagos are more frequently associated with scientists and Charles Darwin's studies as he developed his theory of evolution, many of the seventeen main islands offer opportunities to surf crystalline waves within this virtually untouched archipelago.

A province of Ecuador, the Galapagos Islands are located more than 500 miles (800 km) from its coast and are open to long-distance swell activity from both the north and the south. The majority of Galapagos surfing is found on the island of San Cristobal, on the eastern edge of this cluster of islands. Here, the coast welcomes waves of between two and twelve feet (0.6–3.5 m) for most of the year.

A handful of the Galapagos Islands' finest spots are centered around Puerto Baquerizo. Tongo Reef and Loberia can produce very good rights and lefts, respectively, but difficult access and hordes of sea lions can make it hard to paddle out. El Canyon is a fantastic left and a favorite wave of those who are allowed to get there by entering the military base or who can boat in, but Carola is generally regarded as the best option around. A long right fronted by a lighthouse, Carola produces round, clear water barrels over a lava rock reef amidst all the marine and wildlife that have given the Galapagos Islands their fame.

Surf Galapagos Islands

Location:
Pacific Ocean

Country:
Ecuador

Language:
Spanish and Quechua

Currency:
US Dollar

The Good . . .
- Clean water
- Amazing marine and wildlife
- Uncrowded

And the Bad . . .
- Difficult access
- Seals
- Lack of nearby hospitals
- Expensive

Left Idyllic Galapagos anchorage at Puerto Ayorra, Isla Santa Cruz.

Right An unidentified rider backs into a down-the-line left at El Canyon.

Key to map
- Tongo Reef
- Loberia
- El Canyon
- Carola

SANTIAGO
SANTA CRUZ
FERNANDINA
ISABELA
SANTA FE
SAN CRISTOBAL
Puerto Baquerizo
FLOREANA
ESPAÑOLA

Northern Peru

La Herradura, Cabo Blanco, Chicama

Surfing is immensely popular in Peru. Besides the fact that the country has generated both male and female world surfing champions, this South American country may have been home to history's first wave riders: ancient Caral, Viru, Mochica, and Chimu fishermen once rode the rolling waves on small craft made of totora reeds known as *caballitos*, which translates to "little horses."

Above Fabricating fishing craft out of totora reeds is an ancient tradition in Peru.

Most of Peru's coastline is perfectly angled to receive the endless lines of south and southwest swells sent up via Antarctica, and the country's extreme north region juts out just enough to allow north swells onto its shores. This wealth of swells makes it possible to find surf in Peru nearly every day, and makes the north the destination of choice.

There are myriad great breaks up and down Peru, the majority of them left point breaks, making this a dream destination for goofyfooters. Waves near Lima, like La Herradura, get very good, but they are also crowded and polluted, so most locals look to the north. Near the Ecuadoran border, outside Piura, left points like Cabo Blanquillo, Los Organos, Máncora, Punta Ballenas, Punta Restin, Punta Arena, and Punta Lobo turn on with north swells from November and March. The world-class wave up this way is Cabo Blanco, a radical, round, draining left tube ride known as the Peruvian Pipeline. The coast halfway between Lima and Ecuador, though, is the reason most traveling surfers come to Peru. This region is blessed with a run of seemingly unending, perfect sand-and-rock left points, including Pacasmayo, Puémape, Punta Prieta, and Punta Huanchaco.

However, there is an even better, longer wave in the middle of it all. Chicama, arguably the world's longest left, has been said to connect exciting, four-minute rides for more than two miles. Surprisingly uncrowded for such a renowned wave, Chicama is undoubtedly top of most serious surfers' to-do lists.

Surf Northern Peru

Location:
Pacific Ocean

Country:
Peru

Language:
Spanish

Currency:
Nuevo Sol

The Good . . .
- Great left points
- Cheap

And the Bad . . .
- Thefts
- No fancy resorts

Key to map
- Máncora
- Cabo Blanco
- Pacasmayo
- Puémape
- Chicama
- Punta Prieta
- Punta Huanchaco
- La Herradura

Right It usually takes a handful of leg-burning waves to make it all the way down the point at Chicama, the longest left in the world.

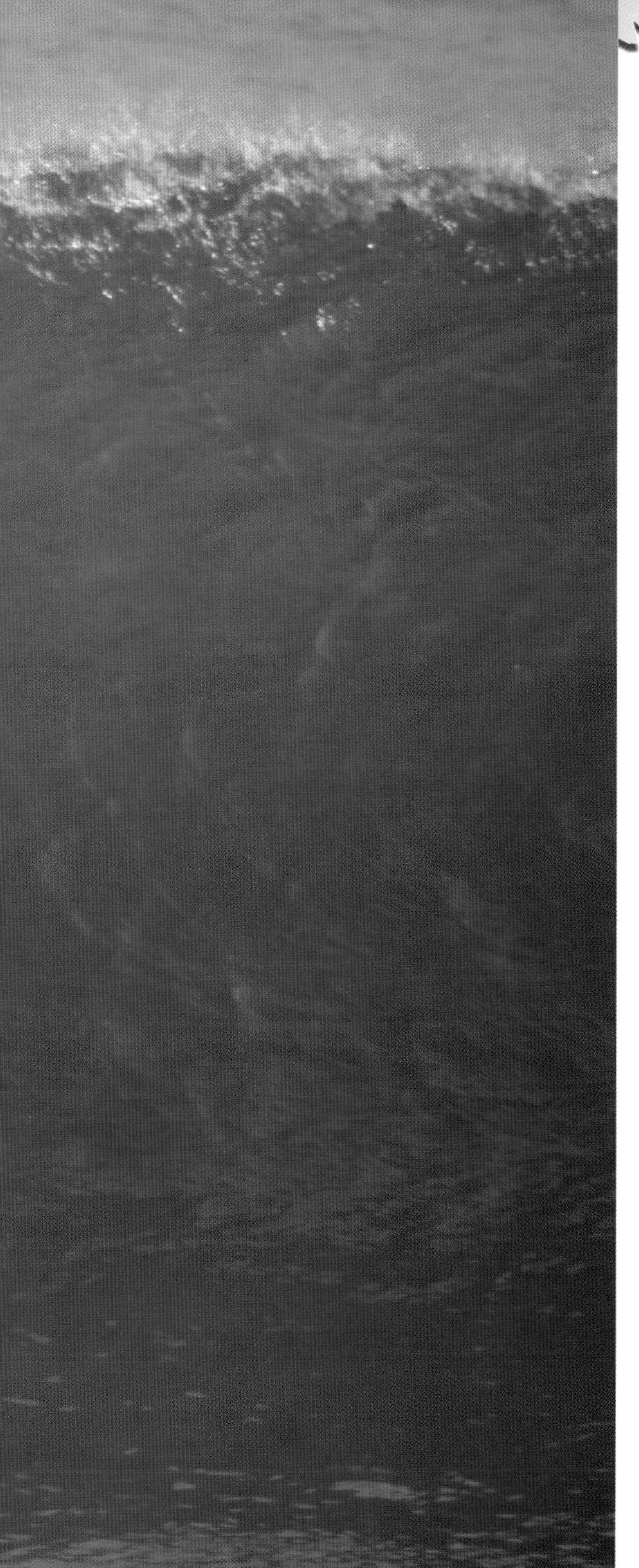

Central Chile

Puertecillo, Pichilemu, Punta de Lobos

Chile has more than 2,500 miles (4,000 km) of Pacific-facing coastline, most of it blessed with rideable waves. Add consistent year-round south and southwest swells, plus an offshore trench that drops to depths beyond 25,000 feet (7,600 m), and the result is an incredibly long stretch of left-hand points and reefs.

Considering Chile's concentration of good waves and close proximity to countries such as Peru and Brazil, which both have extensive surf histories, it is perhaps surprising that Chileans did not begin stand-up wave riding until about 1970. But they have quickly made up for lost time by mapping out a goofyfooter's dream, with enough excellent waves to rival any region on Earth.

While the north and south sides of Chile are as rich in surf as they are topographically different, the main surfing area is found outside the megalopolis of Santiago, home to 10 million of the country's 15 million residents. Near the town of Quintero, classic left point break setups such as El Claron and Papagayo are easily found, as well as the powerful beach break of Ritoque, the historic site of Chile's first ridden wave.

More lefts like La Boquilla and Matanzas can be found outside Navidad, as well as the privately owned peeling, hollow spot known as Puertecillo. Just south is Pichilemu, a very fast, racing left-hand wall with several tube sections, often called Chile's longest barrel. Punta de Lobos, though, is the pick of the litter here. A rock-lined point that is good from three to thirty feet (1–9 m) or more, Punta de Lobos is full of juicy barrels and down-the-line walls. It can handle whatever waves are thrown its way, crafting them into watery works of art.

Key to map

- El Claron
- Papagayo
- Ritoque
- La Boquilla
- Matanzas
- Puertecillo
- Pichilemu
- Punta de Lobos

Quintero

Santiago

Surf Central Chile

Location:
Pacific Ocean

Country:
Chile

Language:
Spanish

Currency:
Chilean Peso

The Good . . .

- Many left points
- Consistent swells
- Friendly locals

And the Bad . . .

- Cold water
- Pollution
- Rip currents
- Wind

Left Famed globetrotting free-surfer Joel Tudor races across the Mirador section of Punta de Lobos.

Riding on the Shoulders of Giants

"The wave commands so much focus and so much attention that it's the only thing that matters."

—Dave Kalama, in *Riding Giants*

South America's Largest Surf

The southern Pacific coastline regularly receives powerful swells from the northern and southern hemispheres. Along with some of the longest waves in the world, this range also contains a number of big-wave venues.

In the bottom quarter of South America, in the long, thin country of Chile, Punta de Lobos reigns as one of the biggest waves in the continent. A left-hand point break capable of five-hundred-yard (450 m) rides and set in picturesque surroundings, it can handle huge south swells of thirty feet (9 m) or more. When it gets large here, serious cold-water currents sweep across the point to make paddle-in sessions somewhat frustrating and definitely dangerous. Nevertheless, scoring some of Lobos's heavy-water waves can make the spaghetti-arms effort more than worthwhile.

Right A lone gunman assesses the scary situation at Punta de Lobos, Chile.
Far right Californian big-wave charger Brad Gerlach races under a heaving lip at El Buey, Chile, as tow-in partner Mike Parsons spectates from a very precarious position.

The Biggest Waves in South America

- Pico Alto, Peru
- El Buey, Chile
- Punta de Lobos, Chile
- Papa Tangaroa, Rapa Nui

Big-wave boards

In 1937, the Honolulu crew of John Kelly, Wally Froiseth, and Fran Heath created crude pintails and stern bottom contours—the precursor to fins—by chopping down the tail area of their finless, ten-foot (3 m) redwood plank boards. Right away, the gang's "hot curl" design eliminated the tendency toward "sliding ass" on steep waves. The inclusion of fins and core materials like balsa and foam in the 1940s and '50s helped craftsmen such as Joe Quigg, George Downing, and Pat Curren establish the next big-wave board templates. Single fins stabilized boards and enabled quick-angle adjustments, and these long, pintail "guns" handled drops and outran rushing whitewater. In the late 1960s and '70s, big-wave guns—like other surfboards—shrank in weight and size, with shapers Dick Brewer and Mike Diffenderfer at the fore of the evolution. Rails were thinned and edge was added in the rear. In a major change in the '80s, Simon Anderson's clustered, three-fin thruster made its way onto big-wave boards, but the nine- to eleven-foot (3 m) guns did not lose length, which was key to harnessing the paddling speed needed to stalk and catch fast-moving swells.

With the advent of tow-in surfing in the '90s, the whole game changed. Now, with the speed provided by personal motorized watercraft, the long guns previously used for paddling in had to be adapted. The result was maneuverable tow-in boards, six to seven feet (1.8–2 m) long, which had foot straps to keep riders fixed, and flat weights in the deck to retain momentum on big waves.

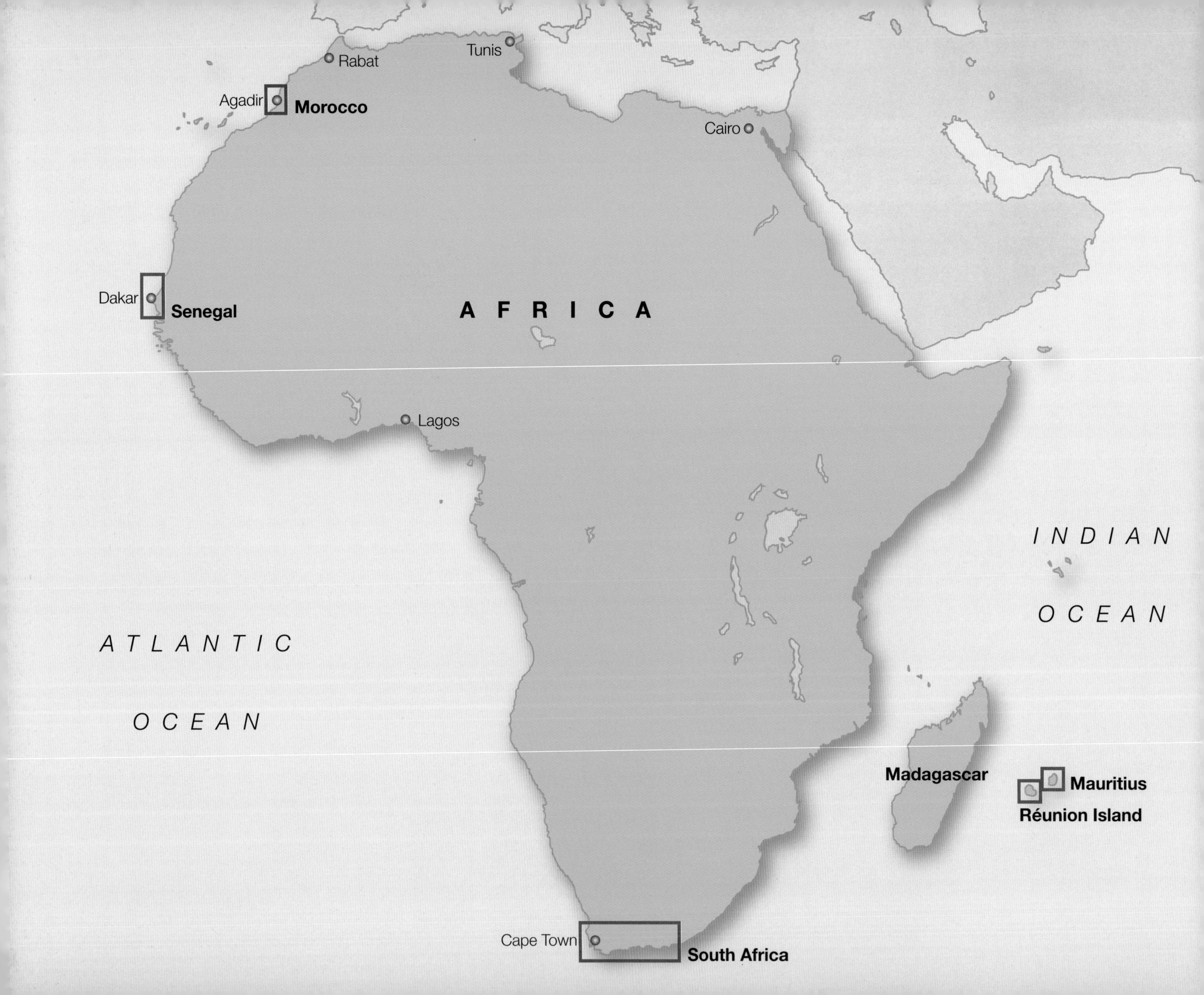
Tunis
Rabat
Agadir
Morocco
Cairo
Dakar
Senegal
AFRICA
Lagos
INDIAN
OCEAN
ATLANTIC
OCEAN
Madagascar
Mauritius
Réunion Island
Cape Town
South Africa

Africa

The vast continent of Africa is home to a wide variety of established surfing areas as well as unexplored gems around its lengthy coastline and on surrounding islands. From the harsh deserts in the north to the equatorial jungles in the central region, to the windblown and cooler climes of the south, the continent is a land of extremes, both in and out of the ocean, where water temperatures range from the mid fifties (13°C) to eighty degrees Fahrenheit (27°C).

The individual surfing histories of countries across Africa are as varied as its terrain. South Africa was first surfed as early as the 1920s; Ghana was surfed initially in the '60s; yet Madagascar's majestic coasts did not attract surfers until the '80s. Local populations of surfers range from over 50,000 participants in some ocean-facing countries to zero surfers in others.

Africa receives swell throughout the year from different oceans and a host of meteorological activities. Low-pressure systems from the North and South Atlantic Oceans, Indian Ocean, Southern Ocean, plus cyclonic activity off both the east and west coasts, provide waves from small and playful to giant and deadly. Some of the best right-hand waves in the world are to be found in Morocco and South Africa, while a few of the best lefts exist on the beautiful, lush, offshore islands of Réunion and Mauritius.

World-class surf aside, the entire west coast of Africa is busy with empty waves. Though often difficult or dangerous to access, the stretch from Senegal to Namibia is a rarely visited run that hides a good deal of untapped gold. There are plentiful waves on the east coast of Africa, too, though swell windows are limited and harsh onshore winds are common. Risks are also plentiful, and include civil war, bandits, impassable roads, floods, and disease. While surfing, be sure to watch out for sharks, hippos, and camouflaged saltwater crocodiles, and steer clear of waters polluted by cities and small villages alike. For most traveling surfers, danger is easily avoided with a bit of research and by applying common sense.

Morocco

Boilers, Anchor Point, Hash Point

On the extreme northwestern tip of the African continent sits Morocco, separated from Europe by the narrow Strait of Gibraltar. Morocco was first surfed in the 1950s by military servicemen stationed in the central region. The area became a staple for traveling European and African surfers and hippies during the heydays of the late 1960s and early 1970s. Today, a stark landscape with steep cliffs and rocky shorelines still provides the backdrop for much of the lineup, with cheap living and generally friendly people adding to the allure for traveling surfers.

Summers in central Morocco are incredibly hot and dry, because the region has many of the same conditions as the searing Sahara Desert, just to the south and southeast. Winters in this part of the country, though, can feel almost tropical, with warm days and sporadic rainfall. And, luckily, it is during Morocco's winter months, especially November through March, that the best surfing conditions are to be found.

Central Morocco is a regular-footer's paradise. A series of excellent right-hand point breaks and reefs dot the coastline from Cape Ghir, home to the fast, hollow waves of Boilers, down to the major city of Agadir. Good waves can be found to the nearby north and south as well, at spots like Immesouane and Boats Point, respectively, but the action found between is more than plentiful.

The Moroccan spot of legend is Anchor Point. Best on medium to big swells, Anchor Point is a vast, top-to-bottom racetrack wall, and it gets even better at ten feet (3 m) or bigger. Though Anchor Point is sometimes broken into sections due to shifting sandbars beneath, when everything lines up this spot becomes a speed run that can connect with Hash Point along the coast to the east, below the village of Taghazout, and dole out rides up to two minutes long.

Key to map

- Immesouane
- Boilers
- Anchor Point
- Hash Point
- Boats Point

Surf Morocco

Location:
Atlantic Ocean

Country:
Morocco

Language:
Arabic and French

Currency:
Moroccan Dirham

The Good . . .
- Right point breaks
- Friendly people
- Uncrowded

And the Bad . . .
- Harsh environment
- Thieves
- Sea urchins
- Rocks
- Black scorpions
- Wind

Brazilian surfer Leonardo Neves stands tall in a round Morrocan barrel at a secret spot on the wild side of Taghazout.

Senegal

N'Gor Rights, N'Gor Lefts, Ouakam

The African Republic of Senegal is a humble yet superior surfing locale, with a tropical climate. Once passed over by international travelers due to internal strife, the country now has a stable democracy and a laid-back, peaceful atmosphere.

Senegal was introduced to stand-up surfing when Bruce Brown, Michael Hynson, and Robert August passed through in 1963 while filming *The Endless Summer*. Of course, it is likely that the locals enjoyed frolicking in the waves on crude mats and belly boards before the crew's arrival. But surprisingly, Senegal still has a tiny local surfing population, nearly fifty years after the sport was first officially demonstrated there–another bonus for traveling wave hunters.

The region's best surfing areas can be found near the capital city of Dakar. Dakar and the Almadies Peninsula, thanks to their unique geography, are open to swells from the south, west, and north, with several surf breaks within walking distance of one another. Senegal is rideable most of the year, with the August-to-October hurricane season providing action from the south, and north Atlantic storms creating the peak surf season from November through May. When onshore wind conditions become problematic, one can easily escape them by simply taking a short trip to spots on the opposite side of the peninsula.

Fun reef and beach-break waves can be found in Dakar proper, but the waters here can get quite polluted. At least a dozen breaks on the peninsula offer a cleaner ride. The tiny island of N'Gor houses two of the most popular spots around, with a right and a left on its west and east edges, respectively. N'Gor Rights is where the duo in *The Endless Summer* found their best rides, and remains one of the top surf spots in Senegal. But it is Ouakam, near the lighthouse, that has become the country's world-renowned wave. A perfect peak tucked inside a cove, Ouakam delivers fast, top-to-bottom, left and right barrel rides after a forgiving takeoff.

Above The African sun closes over N'Gor village. North Carolina standout Jesse Hines takes a bit off the top of a punchy left.

Surf Senegal

Location:
Atlantic Ocean

Country:
Senegal

Language:
Predominantly French

Currency:
CFA Franc

The Good . . .

- Friendly people
- Few surfers
- Inexpensive
- Warm weather

And the Bad . . .

- Pollution
- Scam artists
- Onshore winds
- Urchins
- Disease

Key to map

- N'Gor Rights
- N'Gor Lefts
- Ouakam

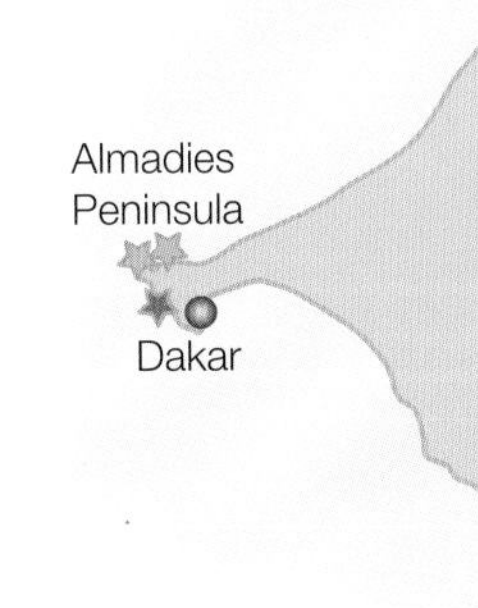

Right American East Coaster Sam Hammer carves a vicious hack into a clean wall at N'Gor Rights.

South Africa

The Hoek, Jeffrey's Bay, Bruce's Beauties

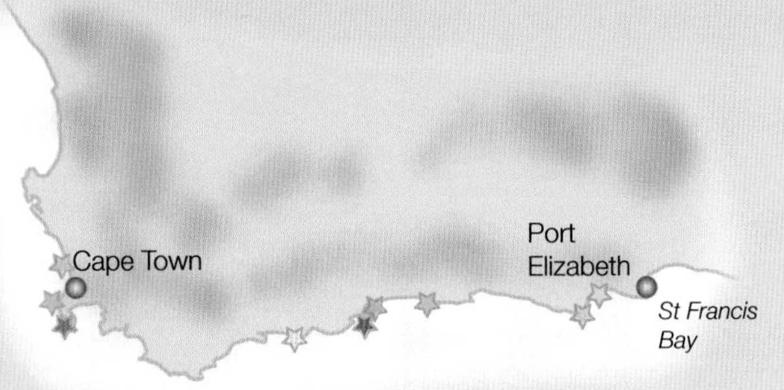

Key to map

- Milnerton
- Dungeons
- The Hoek
- Stillbay
- Mossel Bay
- Outer Pool
- Murphy's
- Bruce's Beauties
- Jeffrey's Bay

Surf South Africa

Location:
Atlantic and Indian Oceans

Country:
South Africa

Language:
English widely spoken

Currency:
Rand

The Good ...

- Natural environment
- Myriad classic point breaks
- Cheap

And the Bad ...

- Great white sharks
- Hippopotamuses and crocodiles
- Sharp mussels

At the base of the continent, South Africa has a wealth of world-class waves, including Africa's richest surf region, Port Elizabeth. This beautiful coastal stretch with mountainous backdrops offers a dizzying number of options–and the globe's best right point break.

Wave riding in South Africa started in Durban in the 1920s, first with belly boarding, followed by stand-up surfing on solid redwood plank-style boards. A respectable surf culture flourished during the following decades, but it was the 1963 visit by filmmaker Bruce Brown, Michael Hynson, and Robert August and subsequent release of *The Endless Summer* that revealed the country's wildlife and relatively untapped surf potential to an international audience.

Best between April and October, when southerly swells march in from the Roaring Forties, South Africa's bounty can keep traveling surfers busy throughout the season. Closer to Cape Town, the full range of wave types can be found, from run-of-the-mill beach breaks at Milnerton to tubes at The Hoek to terrifying drops at Dungeons. Farther east, in a pastoral run that locals call the Garden Route, a couple dozen other prime peaks exist, chief among them Stillbay, Mossel Bay, Outer Pool, and Murphy's.

The St. Francis Bay area, though, is the main attraction. Made famous by the climactic scenes in *The Endless Summer*, the speeding, ruler-edge rights of Bruce's Beauties still dole out delightful days of classic right-hand surf with solid southeast swells, even if spreading developments now sprawl across the once-untouched dunes. Just an eighteen-mile (28 km) drive away, the real South African star, Jeffrey's Bay, was first tested in 1964. The unchallenged champion of right-hand point breaks, Jeffrey's is a jaw-dropping sight when it works to perfection. Incredibly fast, almost mechanical, achingly long, and insanely hollow, this highest of all high-performance point waves usually breaks into five different sections. But, on rare days, some lucky soul is given the chance to complete the entire point with a thrilling three-minute ride.

Below Table Mountain, off Cape Town, can be seen from the west coast on a clear day.

South Africa's coast is littered with semi-secret hideaways. Local charger Mike Schlebach enters a thick section through the back door.

Réunion Island

L'Hermitage, Trois Bassins, St. Leu

Lying in the Indian Ocean some 500 miles (800 km) east of Madagascar, Réunion Island is one of the most idyllic destinations that the planet has to offer. The island is of volcanic origin and sits at a latitude close to that of Tahiti and the rest of French Polynesia. Lush, mountainous, and tropical, the interior of this small island, like Tahiti, is covered with dense rain forest. The island is governed by France, with the same status as its mainland regions, and most of its towns are scattered around its approximately 125 miles (200 km) of coastline.

Initially tested by traveling surfers in the late 1960s, photographs of the amazing left at St. Leu printed in 1980s surf magazines officially put the island on the world's surf map. Réunion receives swell activity throughout the year from a combination of tropical storms and groundswells pushing north from the southern Indian Ocean. Best between June and August, these groundswells provide the top surf conditions. Most of the best breaks on Réunion are on the western shore, the leeward side of the island, with at least forty different spots, possibly more, between Pointe des Galets and Saint Pierre. At the port of Saint Gilles, nearly two dozen waves can be found, with the hollow rights and epic lefts at L'Hermitage and the super-consistent area of Trois Bassins. However, ever since those first magazine photos appeared, Réunion has been synonymous with St. Leu. A bending left-hand point break that wraps to a near 90-degree angle, St. Leu often starts with a long wall, grows as it runs down the reef over shallow coral, and moves through multiple barreling sections before shouldering off a couple hundred yards later.

Surf Réunion Island

Location:
Indian Ocean

Country:
France

Language:
French

Currency:
Euro

The Good . . .
- Tropical climate
- World-class lefts
- Year-round surf

And the Bad . . .
- Expensive
- Sharks
- Coral

Left A tropical, Indian Ocean sunset ends another glorious day on Réunion Island.

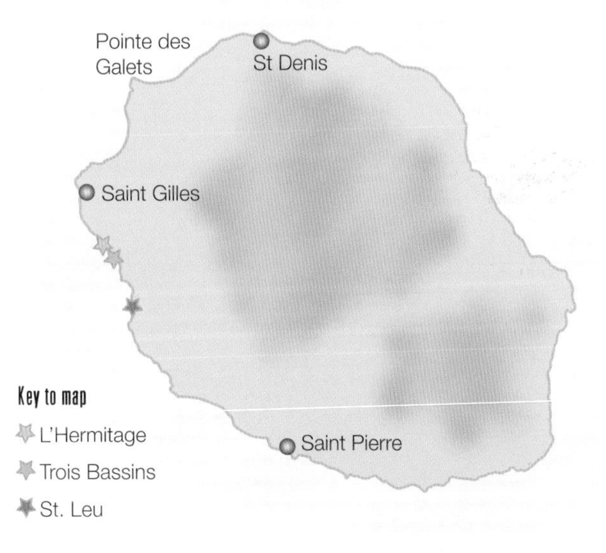

Right Three-time world champion Tom Curren hits the gas pedal through a backside bottom turn at St. Leu.

Mauritius

Souillac, One Eyes, Tamarin Bay

The exotic island of Mauritius lies less than 200 miles (320 km) northeast of Réunion Island, and the two islands enjoy much of the same tropical weather, surf season, and scenery. And, like Réunion, Mauritius is home to one of the world's best left-hand waves.

Mauritius was first surfed in the late 1950s and featured in surf magazines only periodically during the following two decades. The event that gave Mauritius its fame was the legendary mid-1970s release of Larry Yates's surf travel film *The Forgotten Island of Santosha*, and the associated *Surfer* magazine article. Focused on the goal of discovering waves in uncharted lands, Yates's landmark movie was centered on a mystical, unnamed island, its ancient culture, and a perfect, empty wave called Santosha.

Mauritius has more than one surf break, however; in fact there are nearly twenty good breaks. Souillac, a left point break, is arguably the best spot on the island's south shore. A pair of long, left-hand reef pass waves on the southwest corner, Passe de l'Ambulante and One Eyes, are accessible by a short boat ride. But it is Tamarin Bay, a flawlessly barreling left that shoots surfers in and out of its inner sanctuary for more than 200 yards (180 m), dangerously close to the shallow reef below, that is the highlight. Tamarin Bay was the feature wave in *Santosha*, shown in its eight- to ten-foot (2.4–3 m) glory in 1974, a moment in history that helped spawn the still-unending search for surfing nirvana.

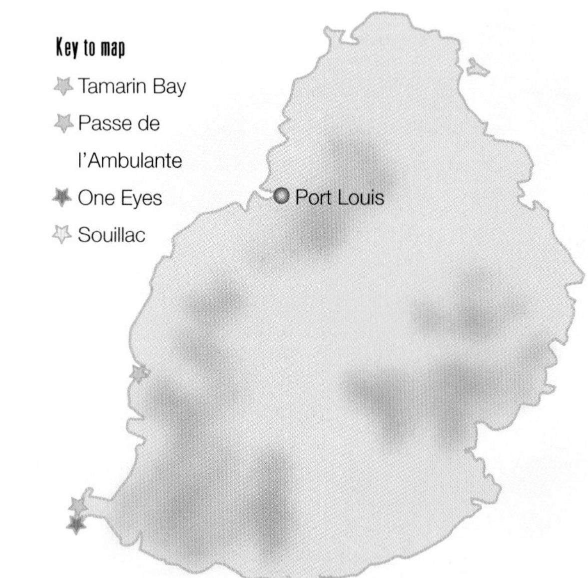

Surf Mauritius

Location:
Indian Ocean

Country:
Mauritius

Language:
English, French and others

Currency:
Mauritian rupee

The Good . . .
- Exotic locale
- Beautiful scenery and beaches
- Warm water

And the Bad . . .
- Shallow coral reef
- Cyclones
- Sharks

Left A sea-borne view of Mauritius, across invitingly warm, turquoise water.

Left Flawless lefts and grooming offshore winds make for a classy day at Tamarin Bay.

"Waves are not measured in feet and inches, they are measured in increments of fear." —Buzzy Trent

The Atlantic Answers the Big-Wave Call

Early on, much of the big-wave attention was focused on the Pacific Ocean, but the Atlantic Ocean is producing just as much awe-inspiring surf. The African big wave found at Hout Bay, in Cape Town, Africa, was the first Atlantic addition to the map.

Dungeons, the result of massive low-pressure systems originating off Antarctica, is the Atlantic Ocean's best-known big-wave venue. An intimidating, thundering right-hander that breaks somewhat frequently between April and October, Dungeons provides steep peaks and racing walls with occasional barrels. On the down side, though, it is also home to great white sharks and freezing ocean temperatures.

First surfed by locals Pierre De Villiers and Peter Button, who paddled into its monster waves in the early 1980s, before the introduction of tow-in surfing, Dungeons has been the venue for the annual Red Bull Big Wave Africa contest since 2000. Since some of the world's best big-wave riders gather at Dungeons yearly, the break has also served as a launching pad for a host of big-wave reconnaissance missions around the Cape of Good Hope; unfortunately, most of those new discoveries have been kept confidential to date.

Riding on the Shoulders of Giants

Red Bull Big Wave Africa

Launched in 1999, Red Bull Big Wave Africa (RBBWA) officially began in 2000, when waves finally reached the requisite height to run the contest. Each year, the world's big-wave chargers are alerted weeks, or even months, in advance, so they can watch the forecast and be ready to descend on Dungeons when the surf grows to a clean fifteen feet (5 m) or more.

- 2000—Sean Holmes
- 2001—Not Run
- 2002—Not Run
- 2003—Greg Long
- 2004—Not Run
- 2005—Not Run
- 2006—John Whittle
- 2007—Not Run
- 2008—Grant "Twiggy" Baker

Left Grant "Twiggy" Baker paddles himself into the history books at Dungeons during the 2008 RBBWA event.

Above right Twiggy drops in on a bomb at Tafelberg Reef, South Africa, and wins the 2008–'09 Billabong XXL Biggest Wave Award.

Measuring waves

In surfing, the measurement of wave heights is almost always cause for spirited debate. Calculating surf from two to twenty feet (up to 6 m) remains an approximate science, but gauging the height of big waves ridden today is a much clearer process.

Scientifically, wave heights are measured in the open ocean, where the average size of a set of waves is counted as the distance between the troughs and crests as they pass a stationary point. When waves approach landfall, though, measuring them becomes more difficult.

Many determine wave height by loosely following the scientific lead, where the face of an individual wave, from trough to crest, equals its size. This is often called the Californian Scale. The Hawaiian Scale—which became prevalent in the mid-twentieth century because of the importance of Oahu's powerful west and north shore surf in the sport—measures height on the back of a wave, from flat sea to its toppling crest. Whether it was created to undervalue heights in hopes of keeping haole surfers away or as a local tactic to gain psychological advantage over outsiders is not known, but the Hawaiian Scale is still used today. Even more confusing are the popular yet vague measurements such as "waist-high" or "double-overhead," used by surfers and surf forecasting websites. For example, a wave approaches the beach and is caught by a surfer. The rider is slightly crouched in her stance, and, as she moves across its face, the top of the wave is just barely visible. A California surfer says the wave is five feet high, a Hawaiian says it's two feet, and a third spectator calls it a "head-high wave."

Measuring surf over twenty feet (6 m), though, has become more universal. Thanks to serious, yearly contests like the Billabong XXL Global Big Wave Awards, photos and video clips of the biggest waves ridden during set periods of time are submitted to a judging panel. The judges' formula uses the actual height of the surfers as the measuring stick, then calculates the wave's height, from trough to crest.

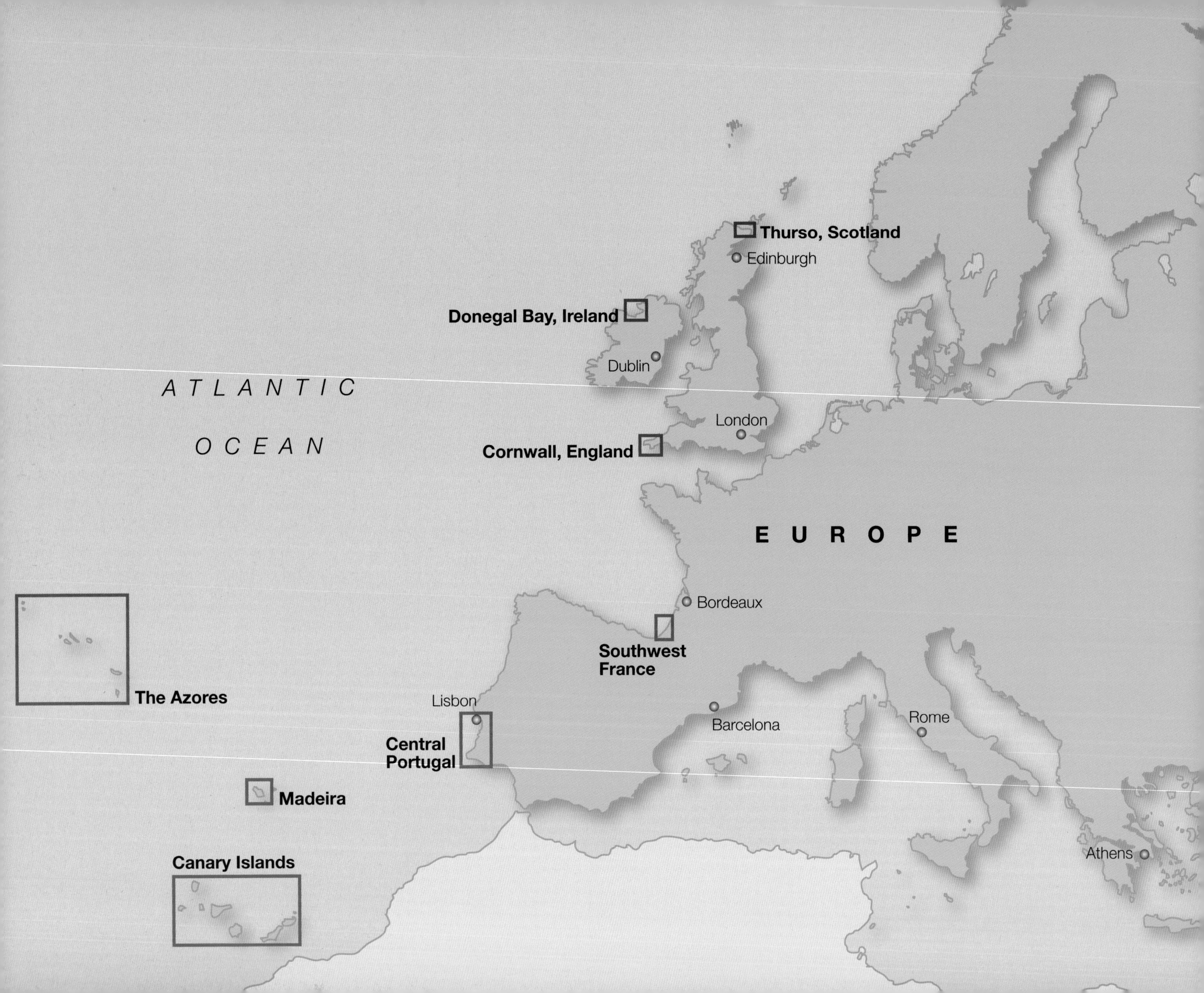

Thurso, Scotland
Edinburgh
Donegal Bay, Ireland
Dublin
ATLANTIC
OCEAN
London
Cornwall, England
EUROPE
Bordeaux
Southwest
France
The Azores
Lisbon
Central
Portugal
Barcelona
Rome
Madeira
Athens
Canary Islands

Europe

Open to year-round swells from the intensely active North Atlantic Ocean, the crooked coastline of western Europe, running from Norway down to Spain, offers a thick array of waves and encompasses numerous island chains, including the Azores, Canaries, and Madeira. The area is home to a wide variety of wave types, from mushy little rollers to some of the planet's biggest surf, and a host of stellar setups between these extremes.

The surfing histories of these European countries and territories are varied. In most of them, stand-up surfboard riding started in the late 1950s and early '60s. It was first introduced by traveling Americans and Australians, then supported by a few enthusiastic locals. While the sport soon flourished in the southern climes with their warmer waters, it took the advent of well-made, full wetsuits for the potential of Europe's surf scene to blossom. This technological development opened the door to the magnificent coldwater breaks of shores like those of Ireland and Scotland.

As European shores depend on the North Atlantic Ocean for their waves, European surfers are lucky that this ocean is a serious storm-making machine, peaking between October and April. Wave heights generally top out at about six to eight feet (up to 2 m) during the winter season. Mega swells carrying fifteen to twenty foot [4.5–6 m] bombs do enter the region a few times each year and, if conditions cooperate, trigger big-wave venues like Mullaghmore Head, Aileen's, The Cribbar, Belharra, and Madeira's Jardim do Mar.

Ocean creatures pose little danger to surfers here. Jellyfish stings and urchin spines are about the extent of it. Unfortunately, polluted ocean waters can be a serious health hazard. But thanks to environmental organizations, governments are slowly being persuaded to consider the safety of Europe's surfers and recognize that their oceans and seas are not empty even when the water temperatures drop.

Thurso, Scotland

Brimms Ness, The Spur, Thurso East

Images of Scotland–vast green moorlands, a rugged shoreline, freezing ocean temperatures, gloomy gray skies, and stiff winds–were once enough to deter curious surf travelers from exploring these ancient lands, but advances in wetsuit technology during the past couple of decades have opened the door to a whole new world of stunning Scottish waves. Well over a hundred named breaks can be found around Scotland and its offshore islands, and, with fewer than 2,000 national surfers, many of these remain empty even when the waves are pumping.

Surfing was reportedly pioneered in Scotland in 1968 by a native teenager, Andy Bennetts. But the ice-cold ocean and cutting winds served as obstacles that kept wave-riding numbers low until more recent decades. Protective gear such as watertight, thick (5 mm) wetsuits, a hood, booties, and gloves has proved the key to unlocking many of Scotland's finer winter spots.

While a great variety of wave regions exist in Scotland, the fifteen or so main breaks are within reach of the town of Thurso, on the far northern shore. These garner the most attention, and with good reason, for the swells that hit the north shore are at their best when they originate in the intense, North Atlantic systems that throw good waves this way between fall and spring. The biggest waves, turning on the shore's flagstone reefs and point breaks, are generated during the dark winter months, when the water is at its coldest.

At Ushar Head, Brimms Ness grabs any swell around and offers a couple of lineups of barreling, shallow right-hand point waves, as well as a longer left point break. East of Thurso, around Dunnet Bay, slab left reefs like The Spur, Nothing Left, Silos, and The Pole can wedge up dredging barrels with enough swell, although getting to them can prove frustratingly difficult. When waves roll into Thurso Bay, though, the slate right reef known as Thurso East, Scotland's finest spot, opens its arms to locals and visitors with perfectly round tubes and fast, extended right-hand walls.

Right Barrels like this will almost make you forget about Scotland's chilly water and winds—for a moment, at least.

Surf Thurso

Location:
Atlantic Ocean

Country:
United Kingdom

Language:
English

Currency:
British Pound

The Good . . .
- Great waves
- Stunning scenery
- Friendly local people

And the Bad . . .
- Cold water
- Harsh weather
- Dounreay nuclear reactor

Key to map
- Brimms Ness
- Thurso East
- The Spur
- Nothing Left
- Silos
- The Pole

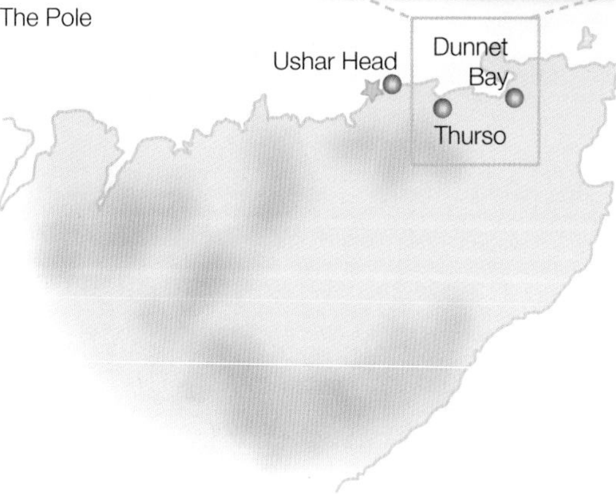

Right Marcelo Trekinho of Brazil pulls into a dredging, hollow right at The Bowl of Brimms Ness, careful to avoid a surfer who happens to be in precisely the wrong place.

Donegal Bay, Ireland

Kilcummin Harbor, Bundoran, Easky

Ireland is a catcher's mitt for Atlantic swells. With myriad wave breaks that pound its north, south, and west coasts, the Emerald Isle's expanse of headlands, craggy bays, and sandy beaches is home to a great deal of surfing terrain and a handful of world-class spots.

Ireland's surfing roots were planted in the early 1960s, but the number of surfers riding Irish waves today is still only about 5,000, a testament to the country's low population and difficult coastline characterized by its hard-to-access breaks. However, an alluring blend of beautiful landscapes, friendly locals, the country's rich culture, and a safe environment–not to mention the epic waves–have lured an increasing number of foreign wave-seekers to Ireland's shores over the last two decades. Steady media coverage of these dreamy, North Atlantic waves will no doubt ensure that the trend continues. Donegal Bay, found on the island's northwestern shore, is one of the best areas for high-quality surf. Wave options abound in Donegal, including the popular beach break peaks of Tullan Strand, the excellent point-style lefts of Kilcummin Harbour, and the rocky-bottomed left-handers of Bunatrahir Bay. But the two best surf areas in Donegal Bay are Bundoran and Easky. The Peak, or simply Bundoran, is a reef break that works both ways but has better lefts, which, on a lower tide, really line up and barrel along the edge of the bay. In Easky, a pair of stellar spots can be found beneath castle ruins. The first is Easky Rights, which creates fast, hollow, tubing walls over a flat reef and is often blessed with offshore winds. The second, on the other side, is Easky Lefts, which mirrors the Rights, with the benefit of easier access and greater consistency.

Surf Donegal Bay

Location:
Atlantic Ocean

Country:
Ireland

Language:
English and Irish

Currency:
Euro

The Good . . .
- Friendly locals
- Variety of waves

And the Bad . . .
- Vile weather at times
- Cold water
- Onshore winds
- Expensive

Key to map
- Bunatrahir Bay
- Kilcummin Harbour
- Easky
- Bundoran
- Tullan Strand

Donegal
Donegal Bay
Sligo

Left Low tide in the town of Bundoran reveals a sampling of the flat, verdant reef the region is known for.

Right Ian Battrick, from the Channel Island of Jersey, locks into an emerald gem at a secret reef in Donegal.

Cornwall, England

Harlyn Bay, Fistral Beach, Porthleven

Surfing has gained a passionate following in Britain since the sport was popularized in the late 1950s in the Cornish town of Newquay (today the country's surf capital) by lifeguards riding their hollow paddleboards in the waves. The 1,100 miles (1,800 km) of coast around the rugged southwest peninsula is dotted with hundreds of surfing beaches, with some of the best breaks to be found in the far southwest, particularly Cornwall.

Protruding into the North Atlantic Ocean, the Cornish peninsula attracts northwest and southwest swells that keep the beaches working for most of the year. September through March is the high surf season for the entire north coast, with waves generally running between two and ten feet, although uncooperative winds are always the major concern.

The bulk of the spots in Cornwall are beach breaks, and there are a lot of them. Some better known and better formed stretches include Sennen Cove, Chapel Porth, Porthtowan, St. Agnes, Penhale, Harlyn Bay, Widemouth Bay, and Crooklets. Newquay's Fistral Beach, for good reason, is considered Britain's premier surfing fetch and is the heart of England's surf culture. North, South, and Little Fistral are all very consistent, work on any tide level, and can lay out classic peaks and walls with a variety of incoming swell directions. Surfers here can be competitive.

Around the southern cape, though, is Porthleven, one of the few stellar reef breaks in the region. A steep drop leading to a bowling barrel and lined-up right, Porthleven gets its perfect shape from the jagged rocks below and attracts crowds of eager surfers when it really starts pumping.

Surf Cornwall

Location:
Atlantic Ocean
Country:
United Kingdom
Language:
English
Currency:
British Pound

The Good . . .
- Vast beach breaks
- Several surf stores
- Friendly locals

And the Bad . . .
- Cold water
- Pollution
- Wind
- Crowds
- Spiny weever fish

Right Big blue tuberide in the United Kingdom: Cornish local Robin Kent rides the wave of the day at Porthleven.

Below Southwest England is littered with wide-open beach breaks such as Harlyn Bay.

RIP CURL

Southwest France

La Piste, Les Culs-Nuls, La Gravière

Not only is the geographically diverse west coast of France blessed with good waves, but it also boasts the longest surf history in Europe, beginning with American screenwriter and novelist Peter Viertel, who brought the first lightweight, Malibu "chip" style surfboard to France, in 1956. With an array of surf-rich regions such as Brittany, Vendée, Gironde, Biscarrosse, Hossegor, Biarritz, and the Côte des Basque, France has plenty to keep the national surfing population of nearly 100,000 happy year-round.

The southwest area of seemingly unending, glistening beaches, though, is one of the most popular places in the country for both local and visiting surfers. Aptly named the Côte d'Argent ("silver coast"), this is a region of clean waves, constantly shifting sandbars, dependable tides, "banana hammocks," and–since it is France–topless sunbathers. The beaches in Hossegor, in particular, have been called the greatest in the world, especially given the north and northwesterly systems that prevail between September and November. Thanks to an offshore trench created by the Adour River to the south, swells funnel into Hossegor and intensify as they approach the long fetch of groomed sandbars.

Many great spots can be found up and down the town beach and to the north and south, each with its own version of the hollow sandbar barrel. La Piste, in Capbreton proper, can produce quick, barreling right and lefts and has earned the nickname VVF, for "very, very fast." Les Culs-Nuls, which plays on the phrase "bare bottoms," rests beyond the shadowing dunes and is known for powerful tubes and perfect shoulders. When big swells enter the equation, surfers bearing guns (long surfboards made for riding big, intense waves) look out to the giant rights of La Nord, past the pounding shorebreak, so long as its bottom contours are favorable. La Gravière is the best of the whole bunch, though, and it is generally thought to be the finest beach break on planet Earth. When the conditions are right, La Gravière receives the trench's channeled energy and folds it into flawless peaks that form gaping, down-the-line barrels mere yards from the high tide line.

Key to map
Les Culs-Nuls
La Gravière
La Nord
La Piste

Côte d'Argent
Hossegor
Capbreton

Surf Southwest France

Location:
Bay of Biscay, Atlantic Ocean

Country:
France

Language:
French

Currency:
Euro

The Good . . .
- Epic beach breaks
- Nightlife
- Sandy bottom

And the Bad . . .
- Crowds
- Rip currents
- Heavily affected by tides

Left An unidentified surfer carves a perfect arc on the face of a La Gravière left.

Right Fashionable French surfmobile—the local choice, a Citroen 2CV, stuffed with shortboards.

Celluloid surf

The surf movie, as surfers know it, was introduced in the early 1950s by Bud Browne, a high-school teacher turned pioneer filmmaker. Not only was Browne's inaugural film—*Hawaiian Surfing Movies*—the first time a big-screen film showed talented surfers performing in their element, but it also established the way this new genre of movies would be shown for the following thirty years. Browne screened his short film in a junior high school auditorium for a one-night run, adding a live narration to the exciting, forty-five-minute montage before a packed house of local surfers.

Browne was joined by a handful of upstart moviemakers over the next two decades, including Bruce Brown, Hal Jepsen, Greg Noll, Walt Phillips, *Surfer* magazine founder John Severson, and Paul Witzig, each adding his own tweak to Browne's surf movie style. For the most part, surf movies of the era held close to the accepted format originally posed by Browne: several quick action clips segmented by shots of popular surfing locations—such as California, Hawaii, Mexico, and Australia—or by the individuals featured, sometimes broken up with things like corny, comedic sketches, surfy cartoons, or similar action-sport sequences such as skateboarding or skiing.

Further mimicking Browne's routine, these movies were shown, with live narration, in beach towns at places like school gymnasiums, town halls, and just about anywhere a makeshift theater could be established quickly and cheaply. Without major studio backing, filmmakers relied on home video cassette recorders, or DVD players, for touring these films across America's coast, especially Southern California, Texas, or the lower East Coast. This practice, called "barnstorming," was the only way to bring films to an audience and for the low-budget filmmakers to recoup their production costs—usually just enough to break even and begin the next venture.

This page Celebrated artist John Van Hamersveld's über-famous poster art for Bruce Brown's *The Endless Summer.*

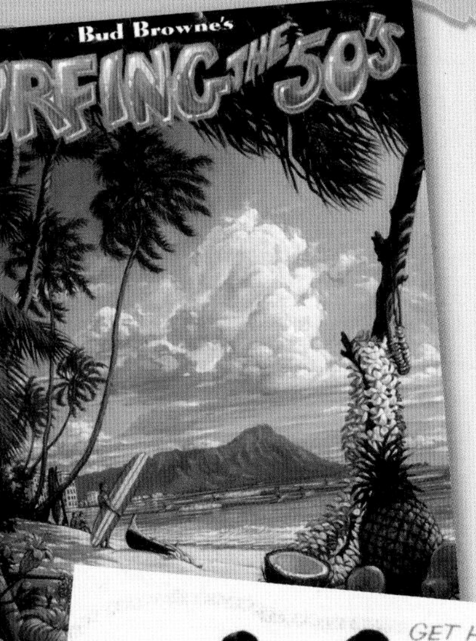

Left *Surfing the 50's* was just one early movie shot, edited, and promoted by surf filmmaker Bud Browne. **Below** A poster for the second offering in the *Gidget* trilogy, *Gidget Goes Hawaiian.*

Left Greg MacGillivray and Jim Freeman's acclaimed film *Five Summer Stories* became the benchmark of action surf movies almost as soon as it hit the screens in 1972.

A NEW PLOT LINE

The first and most notable exception to the plotless surf movie came from Bruce Brown, in 1964. *The Endless Summer*, which followed a pair of surfers seeking the perfect wave across multiple continents and through far-off countries such as Ghana and New Zealand, was a surf film with an actual storyline, and far less surf action than any other before it. Generally regarded by surfers and historians alike as a masterpiece and the best surf film ever made, *The Endless Summer* was met with unmatched success on the barnstorming circuit.

The movie's appeal to surfers and nonsurfers alike led it to be picked up by mainstream studio Columbia Pictures, set into thirty-five-millimeter format, and released in legitimate movie theaters. Worldwide, *The Endless Summer* earned more than $30 million at the box office and was named one of the top ten movies of 1966. Despite the success of *The Endless Summer*, most surf movies stuck to the tried-and-true formula of combining piles of short action clips, accompanied by a soundtrack of popular rock and jazz music. The style has strayed little even today; the main difference between then and now is that in place of barnstorm touring, most filmmakers favor market sales of mass-produced VHS cassettes and DVDs. One new surf movie concept of note, though, is the documentary-style movie, such as *Riding Giants*, *Step Into Liquid*, *Sliding Liberia*, *Between the Lines*, and *Bustin' Down the Door.* These high-quality, historical productions blend real surfing with real life, and have all had a limited theater presence before video sales.

HOLLYWOOD STYLE

Surf movies as Hollywood defines them have a quite different history. Beginning with the 1959 teenybopper film *Gidget*—Columbia Pictures' screen version of Frederick Kohner's best-selling book and Hollywood's first "surf movie"—using the surfing lifestyle as a platform in mainstream movies has continually failed to represent the sport and its dedicated following in any true-to-life manner. More often, these films rely on bad stereotypes and corny dialogue to portray surfers as monosyllabic beach bums, or unsavory types or criminals.

Hollywood has never understood the culture of surfing, nor, it seems, does it care to. Take just a few of the many titles of the 1960s—*Beach Blanket Bingo*, *Surf Party*, *Ride the Wild Surf,* or *Monster from the Surf*—in which flimsy plots have half-naked guys and gals posing as surfers and beach bunnies. These films featured contrived scenes of teens breaking into choreographed song and dance numbers interspersed with studio shots of greasy, smiley characters standing on a surfboard, feet together, with arms waving wildly in the air, in front of surging, giant waves.

Even today, Hollywood has continued to maintain its reputation for cluelessness when it comes to melding surfing and fictional scripts in a credible manner. More recent products such as *Fast Times at Ridgemont High*, *North Shore*, *Point Break*, *In God's Hands*, and *Blue Crush* have still worked the same 1960s lingo and stereotypical behavior into run-of-the-mill, surf-flavored stories.

Right American Hollywood movie actress Sandra Dee smiles for a posed publicity photo during the production of the original 1959 *Gidget* movie in which she starred.

Central Portugal

Supertubos, The Reef, São Lourenço, Coxos

Portugal's coastline is littered with high-quality surf breaks. It is little wonder, then, that Portugal's surf culture has expanded by leaps and bounds over the last few decades. From Viano do Castelo in the north of the country to Faro in the south, Portugal has a thick sprinkling of surf spots and enjoys waves year-round. Portugal consistently offers good surfing conditions during its winter, from October through March, when the North Atlantic Ocean keeps the storm-generating motor running.

Above Portugal's finest pointbreak, Coxos, churns out deep barrels and high-performance walls when clean west and northwest swells arrive.

The central region, which incorporates Peniche, Ericeira, and Lisbon, contains some of the country's finest surf spots. Supertubos, south of the bustling fishing port of Peniche, is one of Portugal's best waves. Supertubos sucks long barrels off its perfect sandbars, complemented by standard offshore winds that groom the surf and, unfortunately, also blow the odor of fish from the local plant into the lineup. Other spots worth checking near here include Molho Leste, Consolaçaõ, and Praia Azul.

The Ericeira stretch is also bursting with top spots, most of them reefs and rocky points. São Lourenço, Crazy Left, Ribeira D'ilhas, The Reef, Pedra Branca, and Foz do Lizandro all get very good, but Coxos is the beauty queen on this stretch of coast. A gorgeous right point break running above a shallow, sharp, rocky reef, Coxos is considered one of Europe's best point waves, and, when it sings, top-to-bottom walls with long, deep tube sections are the norm.

The wealth of surf does not stop in the capital of Lisbon, but extends along the shores to the south. In fact, it was here, at Costa de Caparica, that the first Portuguese surfer, Pedro Martins de Lima, rode waves on his Hawaiian-made koa board. Popular spots here include Praia Corande, Praia Pequena, Praia do Guincho, Parede, São Joao Bolina, Bicas, and Carcavelos.

Surf Central Portugal

Location:
Atlantic Ocean
Country:
Portugal
Language:
Portuguese
Currency:
Euro

The Good . . .
- Myriad breaks
- World-class waves
- Wide swell window

And the Bad . . .
- Wind
- Shallow reef
- Crowds

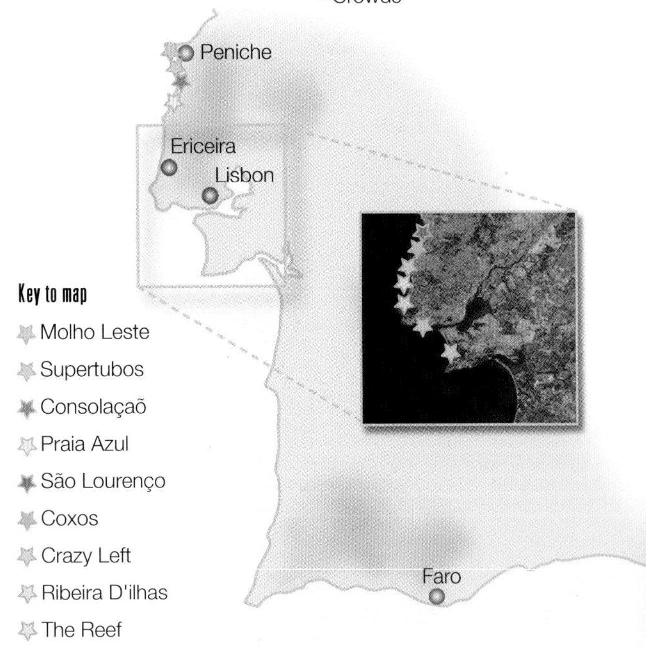

Key to map
- Molho Leste
- Supertubos
- Consolaçaõ
- Praia Azul
- São Lourenço
- Coxos
- Crazy Left
- Ribeira D'ilhas
- The Reef
- Carcavelos
- Costa de Caparica

Right Supertubos boasts consistent offshore winds and peeling sandbar tubes. Just follow your nose to find it.

Madeira

Paul do Mar, Ponta Pequena, Jardim do Mar

The island of Madeira rises out of the Atlantic Ocean a few hundred miles north of the Canary Islands and 350 miles (560 km) west of the Moroccan coast. A beautiful land of vertical cliff walls, lush interior mountains and valleys, and rocky shorelines, Madeira remains a generally quiet place with serious big-wave potential.

A surf stop since the 1970s, Madeira mostly remained a secret garden until a magazine article in the mid-1990s revealed its powerful and shapely waves. Unfortunately for those seeking suntans, there are almost no sandy beaches on Madeira and few, if any, small-wave spots that might be fun for beginners. Most breaks do not even begin to work until the surf is overhead, and waves between ten and twenty feet (3–6 m), or bigger, are the way of things here. This island is mainly for expert surfers only, so if you are in doubt, stay ashore. Clean-up sets can catch you off guard and out of position; if you don't time the waves crashing against the slippery rocks at the shore when entering and exiting, you may find yourself smashed against them or dragged over them.

The southwest section of Madeira garners the most interest from surfers. Three world-class waves within a short driving (or long walking) distance of each other come to life with hefty west-northwest swells, which are best between November and February. Paul do Mar, farthest north, is a big, racy right-hand point tucked beyond a protective sea wall. Inside the next cove is Ponta Pequena, a very hollow, wrapping right that is the most consistent of the three. But Jardim do Mar is the face generally associated with Madeira surfing. Capable of holding the hugest Atlantic juice, Jardim do Mar creates monster, point-style rights with long, clean walls and a few fierce tube sections. Just beware of the occasional boulder along the way and be sure to time your ocean entry and exit perfectly, to avoid getting too intimate with the rocky, unforgiving shoreline.

Above Madeira's volcanic mountain peaks rise vertically out of the North Atlantic Ocean.

Right Striking island scenery, friendly residents, and meaty, hollow surf have caused some to call Madeira the Tahiti of the Atlantic.

Surf Madeira

Location:
Atlantic Ocean

Country:
Portugal

Language:
Portuguese

Currency:
Euro

The Good . . .
- Big point surf
- Friendly locals
- Uncrowded
- Agreeable climate

And the Bad . . .
- Submerged rocks
- Landslides
- Clean-up sets, entering/exiting the breaks

Key to map
- Paul do Mar
- Ponta Pequena
- Jardim do Mar

The Azores

Ponta do Queimado, Contendas, Ribeira Grande, Baixa da Viola

The mountainous, mid-Atlantic archipelago of the Azores is a wondrous set of islands situated about 700 miles (1,100 km) west of Lisbon. Portuguese territories that share their motherland's culture, the nine main islands of the Azores receive incoming swells from almost every direction on the compass.

It is unclear exactly when practices like body boarding and body surfing first began here, but stand-up surfing in the Azores reportedly started with United States Air Force servicemen, stationed on Terceira, in the mid-1960s and early 1970s. Surprisingly, more than forty years later, the number of visiting surfers is still minimal, and access to surf equipment, from boards to wetsuits to wax, is also sparse.

Left A picturesque postcard view of the Azores' trademark coastal, craggy cliffs.

Surf The Azores

Location:
Atlantic Ocean

Country:
Portugal

Language:
Portuguese

Currency:
Euro

The Good . . .
- Small number of traveling surfers
- Variety of waves

And the Bad . . .
- Great white sharks
- Sharp reefs
- Expensive

Key to map
- Villa Nova
- Ponta do Queimado
- Contendas
- São Mateus da Calheta
- Mosteiros
- Rabo de Peixe
- Ribeira Grande
- Baixa da Viola

CORVO
FLORES
GRACIOSA
TERCEIRA
SÃO JORGE
FAIAL
PICO

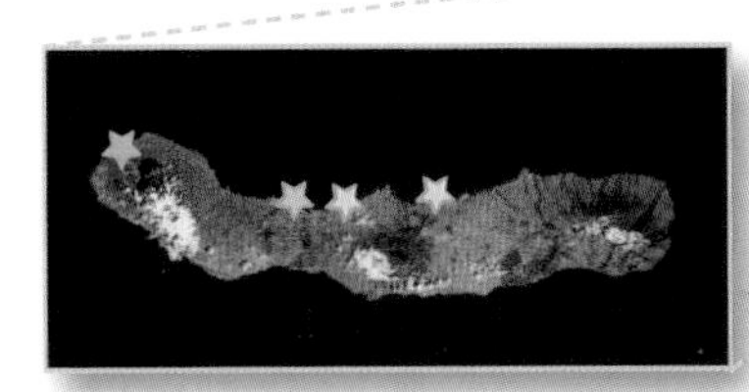

SANTA MARIA

The islands of Terceira and São Miguel form the heart of the Azores surfing scene, despite the presence of rideable waves throughout the chain. With no surrounding continental shelf or barrier reefs, these islands receive raw swells, especially from November to February. It is during these winter months that powerful lines march down from the North Atlantic Ocean and slam the dramatically steep shores to create big, meaty waves at the lava-formed reefs.

Terceira is the most populated and busiest of the Azores islands for surf-seekers, with about a dozen publicized surf spots spread out along the north and east coasts, including the lefts at Ponta do Queimado and Contendas, and right point breaks at Villa Nova and São Mateus da Calheta. The island is also home to the historic capital of the Azores, Angra do Heroísmo. São Miguel, the largest of the islands in the archipelago, draws the most local surfers, and it boasts the best stretch of waves around. On its north shore, four of the finest waves are Mosteiros, Rabo de Peixe, Ribeira Grande, and Baixa da Viola, which range from tame beach breaks to massive and exhilarating, right and left reef breaks strictly reserved for roughneck wave riders.

Above Curvaceous, overhead lines roll across the beach break at Monte Verde, on the island of São Miguel.

Canary Islands

Boca del Abajo, Morro Negro, El Quemao

Lying fifty-five miles (90 km) west of Morocco, the volcanic Canary Islands have become a popular surfing destination since its waves were first ridden in the late 1960s. A small Spanish chain often referred to as the "Hawaii of the Atlantic," the Canaries offer favorable winter weather and ocean temperatures plus impressive, powerful reef waves.

All of the seven main Canary Islands hold surf, but Lanzarote, the easternmost, is often considered the best and gathers surf during much of the year onto its twenty or so named breaks and countless secret spots. Some say that surf can be found in nearly every nook in the island's 100 miles (160 km) of coastline at some time during the changing swell seasons, but the finest breaks, and the heart of the Lanzarote surf scene, is located between La Coleta and La Santa. Best in the dead of winter, November through February, when north and northwest waves appear, this tight stretch gets stout. For peaky rights and lefts that can get big and rough, try Ghost Town; or, if you prefer a classic, left-hand, point-style wave with a well-defined paddling channel, Boca de Abajo is an excellent option.

Farther southwest, Morro Negro is, perhaps, the Canaries' best right–a long, powerful reef break that can handle swells beyond twelve feet (3.5 m) and still hold perfect form. La Santa Left, better known as "The Slab," sitting across the bay from Morro Negro, is a heavily localized, dredging peak that sucks up quickly off an extremely shallow reef. El Quemao, though, is Lanzarote's trademark break. A very hollow, top-to-bottom left-hander that stands up just off the harbor, El Quemao, once known as "Village Left" because of its close proximity to La Santa, is a fearsome barrel that many call the Canary Pipeline.

Surf Canary Islands

Location:
Atlantic Ocean

Country:
Spain

Language:
Spanish

Currency:
Euro

The Good . . .
- Variety of waves
- Warm weather

And the Bad . . .
- Shallow reef
- Difficult coastal access
- Sea urchins

Key to map
- Ghost Town
- Boca del Abajo
- Morro Negro
- La Santa Left
- El Quemao

LA PALMA
TENERIFE
LANZAROTE
FUERTEVENTURA
GOMERA
HIERRO
GRAN CANARIA
MOROCCO

Far left Puerto Rico's Otto Flores cranks a bottom turn on a grinding left at El Quemao, the Atlantic's answer to Pipeline.

Left Four reef breaks seemingly blend into one on a very big swell at Lanzarote's Mirador del Rio.

"You can't catch a freight train on a bicycle, you have to match power with power. Voilà! Tow surfing is born." —Darrick Doerner, from *Stepping into Liquid*

Europe goes XXXL

In the North Atlantic, Europe's giant surf is finally making headlines, with an array of exciting big waves of unknown potential found between Scotland and Spain, albeit all in cold-water conditions.

Considered Ireland's finest big wave, Mullaghmore Head is a frightening, towering left, where, in 2007, record-breaking sixty-foot (18 m) surf was ridden by tow-in surfers. Ireland is also where Aill Na Searrach, also called Aileen's, breaks. Set beneath magnificent Cliffs at Moher, Aileen's was first attempted by tow-in surfers as recently as October 2005. The lucky surfers, who were swung into the giant walls and through screaming, oval-shaped barrels, were John McCarthy, Robin Kent, Dave Blount, and the young, big-wave veteran Rusty Long.

Belharra, just over a mile (2 km) outside Saint Jean De Luz, is probably Europe's most-talked-about big-wave spot. Though it rarely happens, the site saw swells of sixty feet (18 m) in 2003. The vast ocean trench preceding the French reef here allows raw, unfettered ocean swells to leap skyward and form frothing left-handers as they unload onto this offshore shoal.

Riding on the Shoulders of Giants

Europe's Biggest Waves

- Aileen's, Ireland
- Mullaghmore Head, Ireland
- The Cribbar, England
- Belharra, France
- Guethary, France
- La Nord, France
- Cabo Silliero, Spain
- Izaro, Spain
- Playa Gris, Spain
- Jardim do Mar, Madeira

The big-wave wipeout

Big-wave wipeouts are vicious beatings. Whether you are paddle-in surfing or tow-in surfing, falling on a wave measuring twenty to seventy feet (6–20 m) tall is a life-or-death experience—one that takes every ounce of energy to escape from. It is an event where time stands still, turning the painful ordeal, which lasts only seconds, into eternity.

In a usual scenario, the surfer freefalls into the trough of the gigantic wave, skipping down the face until tons of swirling white water collapse and drive him or her into the reef below, or to fathoms of forty feet or more. Some big-wave surfers have described these harrowing moments as being shaken like a rag doll in a dog's mouth or tossed around inside a giant washing machine, getting whipped about so intensely that it feels like your arms and legs could be ripped off your body, experiencing intense water pressure that can blow eardrums, and having several dump trucks simultaneously drop dirt loads on your head. And this is only the first half of the struggle.

Once the tumbling effect subsides, it is often too dark down there to see any semblance of daylight, so quickly figuring out which way is up is paramount. This immediate priority is followed by the imperative to fight to the surface for a gasp of beautiful air, hopefully before the next wave of the set bears down and repeats the nightmare anew. For many big-wave surfers, safely reaching the surface in time means grabbing their leash and climbing up it to the tombstone surfboard bobbing above, knowing it is probably their only chance of survival.

Left Irish surfing legend John McCarthy drops in on a Celtic monster at Aileen's, a spot he helped put on the map.

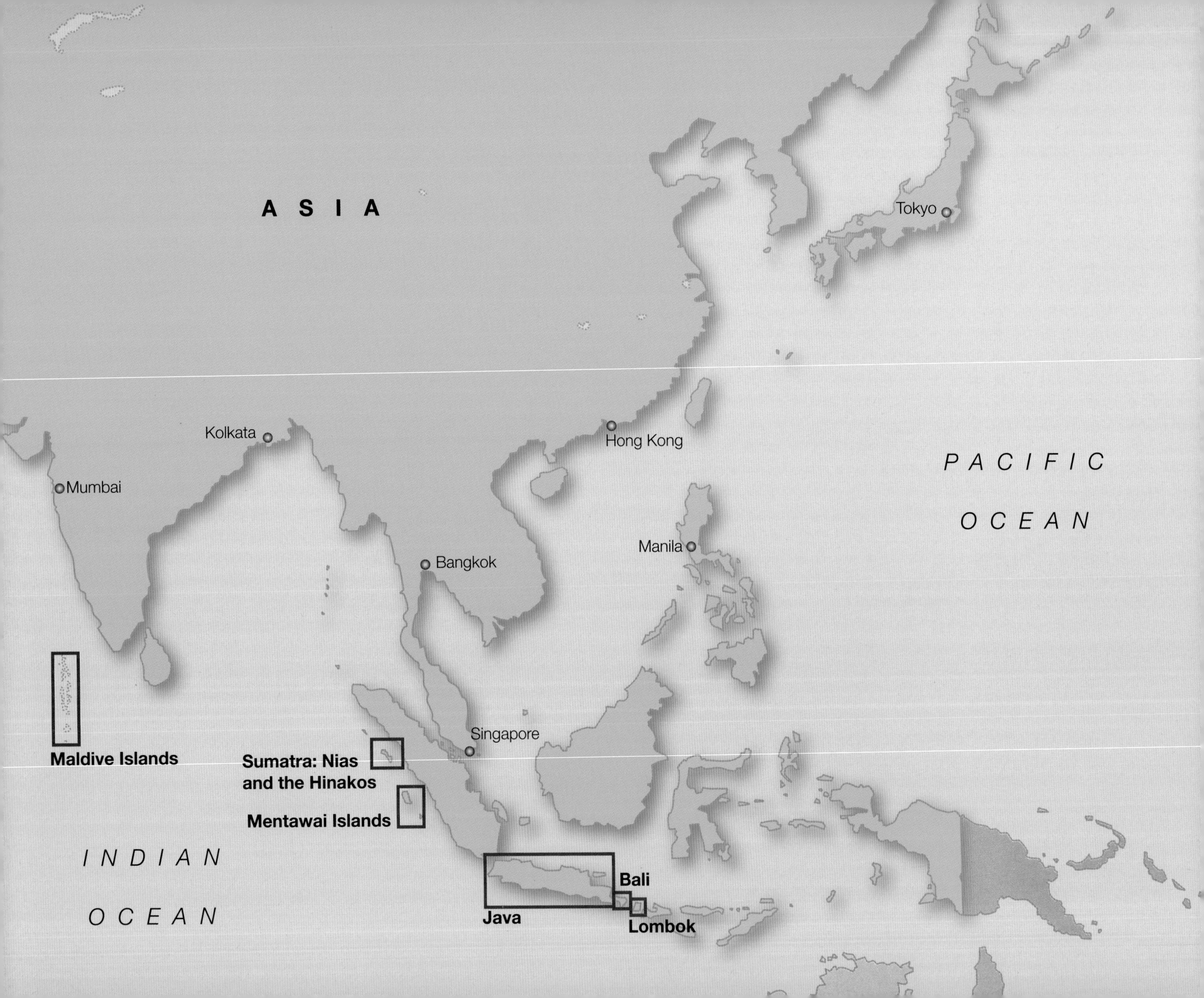

ASIA
Tokyo
Kolkata
Hong Kong
Mumbai
PACIFIC
OCEAN
Manila
Bangkok
Singapore
Maldive Islands
Sumatra: Nias
and the Hinakos
Mentawai Islands
INDIAN
OCEAN
Bali
Java
Lombok

Asia

A cornucopia of wave breaks exist across Asia, with some of the best to be found on the islands situated off the continent's southern and southeastern shores. The fantastic wave-riding territory of these locales was discovered by eager, world-class surfers in the early 1970s, with Bali, Indonesia's island paradise, the first surf destination to be unearthed. Riders subsequently found superlative surf spots in the rest of the archipelago and all the way to the Maldives. New waves are continually being added to the list of prime surf spots in this region, so there are always new gems to ride.

The breadth of Asian waves is vast, and the area's island exoticism is almost as varied. This huge area of ocean includes the pristine, often-deserted islets of the Mentawais, off Sumatra, and the low-lying coral reefs of the Maldives. Reaching these remote islands can be an arduous and expensive task, but the blue gold at the end is worth the journey.

This is the land of the first all-inclusive surf camps and weeklong charter boat surf excursions. If the waves were of a lesser quality and consistency, exclusive resorts such as these would not have survived. Instead, they are thriving, with spaces often booked out from months up to a year in advance. The allure? The beauteousness of the breaks and the warmth of the Indian Ocean.

However incredible the waves, there is still a host of dangers, seen and unseen, lurking in this part of the world. Sharp, shallow, coral-encrusted lava reefs are beautiful and ancient formations that create the perfect form of the waves in this region, but they also rip skin and bone from those riders with harsh wipeouts. Sharks and tigers abound in these waters, though attacks are rare. Polluted ocean waters due to sewage, along with the destruction of natural "filters" like tropical forests and mangroves, are a problem. Disease, sea pirates, and terrorist threats, as exemplified by the 2002 and 2005 bombings in Bali, are also hazards. For the most part, though, traveling well-equipped with medical supplies and exercising a little discretion will ensure a peaceful and life-enriching ride in some of Asia's perfect surf.

Maldive Islands

Honky's, Sultan's, Pasta Point, Chickens

The Maldive Islands make up one of those destinations surfers dream about, conjuring images of luxury resorts, turquoise waves wrapping around tiny, white-sand islets, boats zipping across crystal-clear bays, and thin-lipped, warm-water barrels.

The North Malé Atoll, in particular, is one of the best surfing regions along the Maldive Ridge, which extends nearly 500 miles (800 km). As the story goes, the surf potential of North Malé was discovered by a pair of Australian surfers, Tony Hinde and Mark Scanlon, who ended up stranded on one of the islands in the early 1970s. The duo tested the waters before leaving the area, and Hinde returned a year later, surfing Maldivian gems, solo, for more than fifteen years and eventually teaching some of the locals to surf so he would not be out there alone. Hinde built the first Maldivian surf resort, Tari Village, and the rest is history.

North Malé's breaks all face southeast and welcome groomed Indian Ocean swells, which are in top form between March and October. A few of the finer surf spots here include Jailbreaks, Honky's, Sultan's, Pasta Point, Lohi's, and Chickens.

Honky's (a left) and Sultan's (a right) are part of the same reef that wraps around a low-lying island. The great wave at Honky's refracts and bends around the reef edge, and it actually grows as it moves through the inside section, called Fred's Ledge. Located on the other end of the reef, Sultan's can hold the biggest swells around, never closing out, and it offers high-speed runs and extensive tube time as the wave moves you through its paces. Pasta Point fronts the main resort island and offers long, hollow lefts with high-performance walls. Toward the atoll's eastern point is Chickens, named after the poultry farm formerly found on the island, not for any softness or weakness in its waves. On the contrary, Chickens is actually a very fast and challenging left, with five or more serious tube sections that, on good swells, sometimes link up to form a mind-blowing twenty-second barrel ride.

Right American surfer and writer Michael Kew stalls for a falling lip at Coke's, a fast and challenging wave found in North Malé.

Below Top Australian longboarder Belinda Peterson-Baggs watches a few Maldivians harvest sand from a tiny, uninhabited island. With rising sea levels, locals are trying to reclaim what little land they have.

MALDIVES

Key to map

Chickens · Sultan's · Lohi's · Honky's · Pasta Point · Jailbreaks

NORTH MALÉ ATOLL

Location:
Indian Ocean

Country:
Maldive Islands

Language:
English, Dhivehi or Arabic

Currency:
Rufiya or US Dollar

The Good . . .
- Variety of pristine waves
- Warm water
- Luxury resorts
- Zero pollution

And the Bad . . .
- Shallow reef
- Expensive
- Rip currents

Sumatra: Nias and the Hinakos

Lagundri Bay, Bawa, Asu

Nias, a small island approximately eighty miles (130 km) west of Sumatra, and part of the Indonesian North Sumatra province, is tropical, equatorial, and hot. An exotic land with impressive temples and cheap living accommodations, this island is difficult to reach but well worth the effort.

Nias is yet another superb surf discovery made by Australians. In 1975 John Geisel, Kevin Lovett, and Peter Troy met on a ferry destined for Nias and decided to scout its shores together. What they stumbled upon became known as The Point, more commonly called Lagundri Bay or, simply, Nias. This location turned out to be one of the best right-hand waves on Earth.

The Point at Lagundri Bay is Nias's main break in the south and the island's undisputed champion, though others like Kiddieland and The Machine are nearby. The Point is a perfect right with near-vertical takeoffs, ruler-edge walls, and deep tube possibilities, all tucked into a gorgeous, blue-water nook in the coast. It is, in short, a natural-footer's paradise.

Further exploration of the area led wave-hungry surfers to the tiny Hinako Islands, west of Nias, where two additional stellar surf spots were found. On Bawa, its namesake break is a heavy, outer reef right with an end section that gets downright round and menacing. Ten miles (16 km) from Bawa is Asu, an even smaller island with a fantastic left point that gets big and beastly as it grinds over the reef and around the palm-fringed shore.

Right Iconic freesurfer David "Rasta" Rastovich, nonchalant in a stand-up barrel over extremely shallow reef at a dreamy Hinakos island hideaway.

Surf Sumatra

Location:
Indian Ocean
Country:
Indonesia
Language:
Multiple, including English
Currency:
Indonesian Rupiah

The Good . . .
- World-class waves
- Tropical climate

And the Bad . . .
- Hard to reach
- Malaria
- Crowds

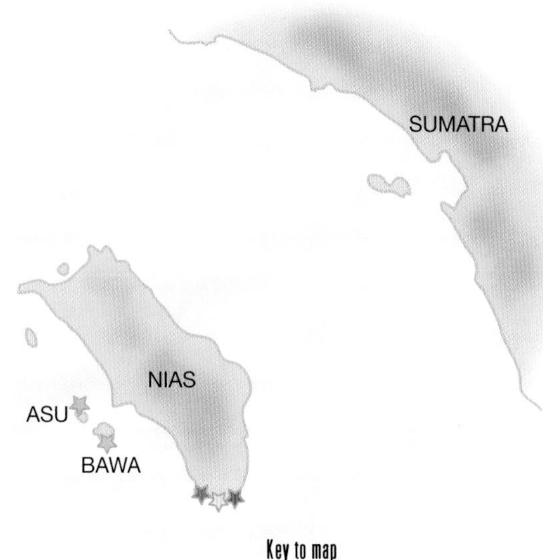

Key to map
- Asu
- Bawa
- The Point/Lagundri Bay
- Kiddieland
- The Machine

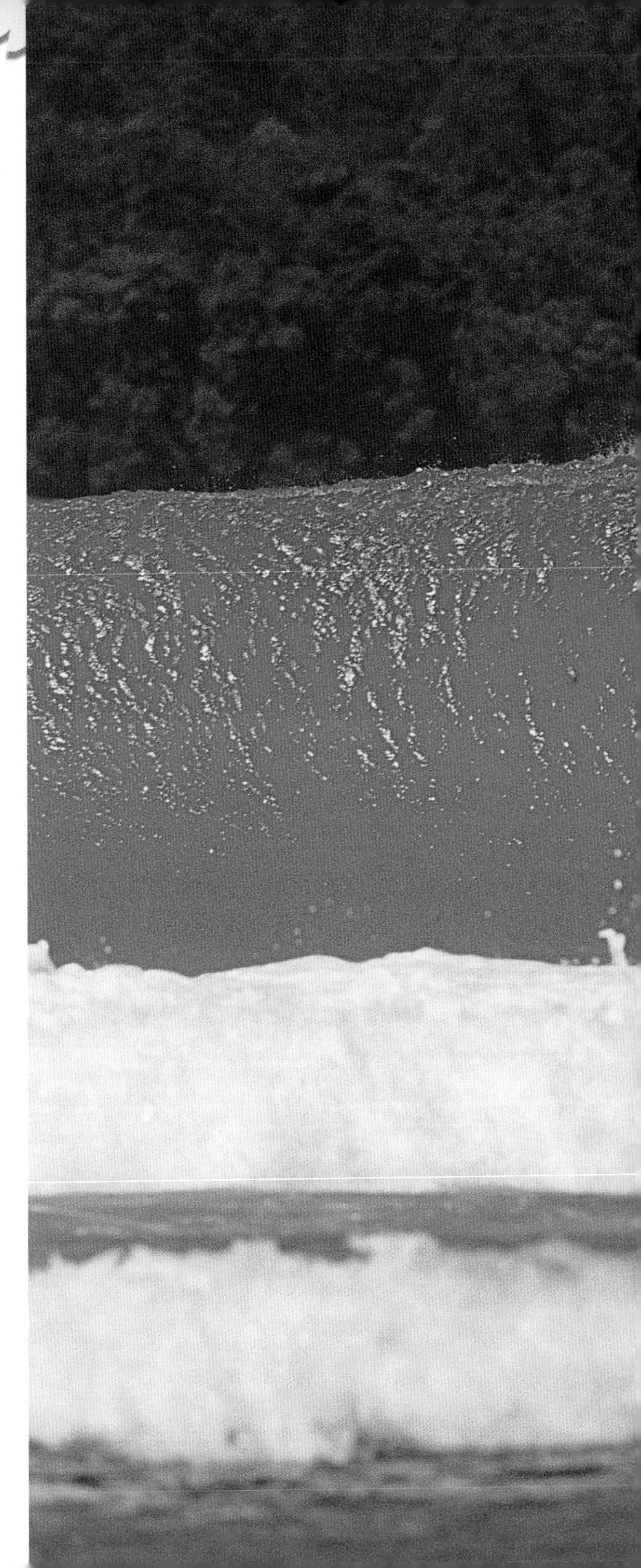

Mentawai Islands

Nipussi, Bank Vaults, Macaroni's, Lance's Left, Lance's Rights

Despite being a relatively recent addition to the global surf map, the Mentawai Island chain, found eighty miles (130 km) west of Sumatra, has quickly become a sought-after wave destination and has also helped change the definition of the dream surf trip.

This run of island jewels was first ridden in 1980, when a small group of Australians boated out from Sumatra, camped for just over a month, and scored pristine waves at a handful of breaks. Astonishingly, word of this amazing wave playground never spread beyond their friends. Almost a full decade later, the now-famous Aussie skipper Martin Daly sailed around the region off and on for more than a year, exploring and surfing the archipelago. Unbeknownst to him, in 1990, New South Wales wave hunter Lance Knight was living wild in the bushes of Sipora, one of the islands, giving names to some of the reefs and riding them alone. By chance, Daly and Knight met while surfing one of the island's fantastic waves–Lance's Rights–and between them they spread tales of the spectacular Mentawai surf over the following year.

Before long, fleets of charter boats were arriving, carrying seven to ten surfers out to the Mentawais for week-long surfing trips. Images of the blue barrels flooded the media and immediately set the area atop every surfer's wish list.

The waves here remain a consistent four to ten feet (1 to 3 m) and bigger, thanks to the steady South Indian Ocean, with the best waves generally occurring from

Left Grab a rail and hold on! Aussie Adam Leslie aims for daylight at Lance's Rights.

Surf Mentawai Islands

Location:
Indian Ocean

Country:
Indonesia

Language:
English

Currency:
Indonesian Rupiah

The Good . . .
- A dream surf destination
- Excellent waves
- Warm and clear water

And the Bad . . .
- Shallow reef
- Reef cuts
- Expensive
- Malaria
- Heat

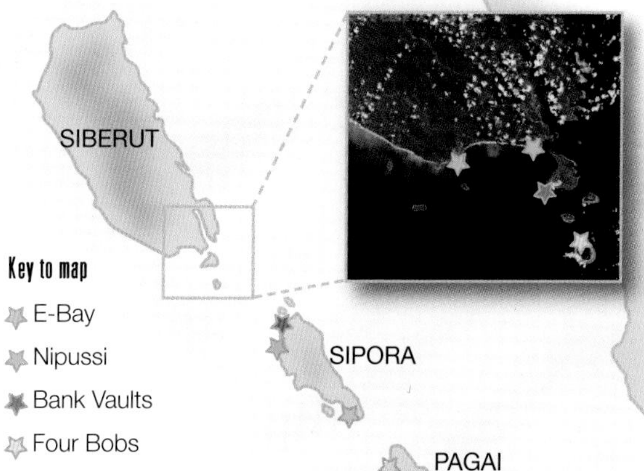

Key to map
- E-Bay
- Nipussi
- Bank Vaults
- Four Bobs
- Telescopes
- Scarecrows
- Lance's Left/Rights
- Bommie Peak
- Macaroni's
- Gilligan's
- Rags Right
- Thunders

March to November. Wind is rarely an issue, but if it does become a problem onshore where your boat is moored, you can simply move around the island.

There is such a great concentration of world-class surf here that many call the Mentawais the richest wave zone on Earth. Spots like Nipussi, E-Bay, Bank Vaults, Four Bobs, Rags Right, and Thunders are just the beginning. Adding to the list, the Banyak Islands and Simulue Islands, north of Nias, hold the goods, too, with less-crowded conditions and even more pristine scenery. Some of the best Mentawai Islands surf is found on Pagai Utara and Sipora. Pagai Utara includes the ferocious big-wave spot Bommie Peak as well as Gilligan's, a more user-friendly wave, but Macaroni's is the biggest lure here. A ridiculously mechanical left with an introductory tube that spins itself into a rippable, high-performance wall, Macaroni's is at its best between three feet (1 m) and six feet (1.8 m) and when every maneuver in the bag, from intense cutbacks to vertical hacks to aerials and beyond, is in play.

The next island north, Sipora, offers a handful of breaks, including Scarecrows and Telescopes, with all types of wave and wind opportunities. Lance's Left, at the island's southern tip, produces long walls and barrels aplenty, with less risk than the waves at Lance's Rights, in the same spot. Lance's Rights, also called Hollow Trees, is the ultimate high-risk, high-reward spot. Round, flawless, fast, mesmerizing tube rides invite confident surfers to have a go at Rights, but beware—a nasty stretch of coral-encrusted lava reef lines the bottom, including a slab known as the "surgeon's table," legendary for sending surfers home with stitches, or worse.

Above Red sky at night, surfer's delight.
Right American Alan Johnson takes a tuberide to its logical limit in the Mentawais.

Surf comic art

The broad genre of "surf art" was born before the advent of surf magazines, when several surfing-themed cartoons were published in the late 1930s and '40s. One of the first was a drawing of DC Comics's crime fighters Superman, Batman, and Robin riding a wave together on the cover of a 1948 issue of *World's Finest Comics*. But it was John Severson who really popularized the cartoons and comics designed by and for surfers, when he included nearly fifteen of his own drawings in the inaugural issue of his self-published periodical, *The Surfer*, in 1960. The same year, a forty-six-page debut issue of *Surfer's Annual* by Greg Noll was printed, featuring cartoon work by a teenaged artist named Rick Griffin. *Surfer's Annual* was short lived, but the talented Griffin began producing cartoons for *Surfer* in 1961, with the imaginative "Murphy" strips. *Surfer* also published a series of Mike Dormer's loveable, beer-swilling "Hot Curl" character panels later in the '60s, as well as a collection of cartoons drawn by magazine readers and run under the title "Surftoons."

SURFING HITS THE BIG TIME

Mainstream newspapers, magazines, and comic books soon embraced the youthful sport, too, most notably in one of Charles Schultz's 1965 "Peanuts" strips, where Snoopy surfs across a wave, sporting a pair of baggy jams and yelling "Cowabunga!" Marvel Comics joined the trend the following year, introducing the intergalactic "Silver Surfer," created by comic legends Stan Lee and Jack Kirby. Explaining the concept, Kirby—known as the King of Comics—revealed, "My conception of the Silver Surfer was a human being from space in that particular form. He came in when everybody began surfing . . . I couldn't do an ordinary teenager surfing so I drew a surfboard with a man from outer space on it."

John Lamb's second surf cartoon, "Rocket 88," created for a spot in *Five Summer Stories*.

Above Rick Griffin's one-off comic book creation, *Tales from the Tube*—the most sought-after surf comic ever.

The superhero—who rides a futuristic surfboard guided by his thoughts while saving Earth from a slew of colorful and inventive villains—graduated to his own title in 1968. A year later, Charlton Comics, which had been catering to the teen crowd since 1951 with *Hot Rods and Racing Cars* and similar titles, launched its short-lived *Surf 'n' Wheels*.

STRIPS, DRUGS, AND ROCK 'N' ROLL

1972 was a busy year for surf cartoons, a creative surge driven perhaps by drugs, the hippy culture, psychedelic rock music or a combination of this and more. In Australia, *Tracks* magazine ran the first "Captain Goodvibes" strip, showcasing a fearlessly bold, often indecent, drunk or stoned surfer drawn by Sydney's Tony Edwards. Captain Goodvibes became an icon of '70s Australian surfing, and even found fame as a radio and animated film star.

Surfing's first animated shorts came from John Lamb, starting with "Secret Spot" in 1972, and then "Rocket 88," in which a dark, white-haired surfer slashes a spearlike board through an unending, color-splashed wave. "Rocket 88" was included in Jim Freeman and Greg McGillivray's surf movie *Five Summer Stories*. Including animated cartoons in surf movies is a style that continues today, in films like *Litmus* and *Sprout* from the 1990s and 2000s.

Another '72 landmark was the twenty-page comic book *Tales from the Tube*: brainchild of Rick Griffin, who was, by then, producing rock 'n' roll concert posters and album covers for bands like the Grateful Dead and the Eagles. The book featured work by Glen Chase, Jim Evans, and Bill Ogden, as well as infamous, often lewd underground Zap cartoonists R. Crumb, Robert Williams, and S. Clay Wilson, and was inserted into an issue of *Surfer*.

Left, from top *Surftoons* featured strips by artists Rick Griffin, Mike Dormer, Nelson Dewey, and Carl Kohler, among others; Silver Surfer first appeared in a *Fantastic Four* Marvel comic in 1966.

Above Surf subculture antihero Wilbur Kookmeyer, created by Bob Penuelas.

Australia's vulgar, irreverent, and crudely cast surf-mag cartoon trend continued, with Mark Sutherland's "Gonad Man" and Steve Cakebread's "Felch" pushing the limits of surf-inspired boorish and dark humor. *Surfer*, though, continued to lean toward the more digestible, witty, relevant, and carefully drawn strips that had started with Rick Griffin's "Murphy" in the early 1960s.

Probably the only other surf cartoon to come even close to the stature and style of Griffin's work initially appeared in *Surfer* in 1986. After cocreating the popular "Maynard and the Rat" strips for the magazine in the early 1980s with partners Rick Bundschuh and Tom Finley, illustrator and writer Bob Penuelas came up with a dorky, wipeout-prone, simpleminded, teenaged everyman he dubbed "Wilbur Kookmeyer," following him through a range of timely situations in a crowded surf world now turned as new age and consumerist as the '80s world around it.

Java

Grajagan, Panaitan Rights, One Palm Point

Java is a surfing holy land, teeming with wave possibilities, friendly people, beautiful and wild surroundings, and surf lore. The south-facing coastline, complete with a deep-sea trench, welcomes those steady South Indian Ocean swells from the east tip to its west tip. Certainly, dozens of different waves dot Java between the Sunda and Bali straits, including classic lefts like Ombak Tujuh and Turtles, and the rare rights at Cimaja Beach. However, it is on the extreme ends of the island that many surfers focus.

Off Java's western edge lies the UNESCO World Heritage Site of Ujung Kulon National Park, on Panaitan Island. Be warned: Panaitan offers no playful, thin-lipped barrels *à la Mentawais*; a run out to Panaitan is serious business. The channel is dangerous; most waves out here are thick, shallow, and heavy; and the island is home to thriving populations of mosquitoes, snakes, sharks, tigers, and even rhinoceroses. But there are incredible tube rides to be had.

Inside the horseshoe-shaped bay, the duo of lefts known as Napalms and Pussies offer less-intimidating, glassy barrels and sections when the pair of points outside are too menacing or windy. These outside points, though, are the reason people go to Panaitan. Panaitan Rights, also called Apocalypse, at the southwest tip, is a steep and heaving barrel with a tendency to pinch riders inside its gaping womb and toss them on to the brutal reef below. One Palm Point covers the island's southern protuberance, peeling long lefts around the corner with perfectly cascading tubes over a punishing reef.

Another Indonesian wave once dubbed the best on Earth is Grajagan. It was first surfed by American wave hunter Bob Laverty and Aussie Bill Boyum in 1972, after both men island-hopped from Bali to find the mythical left that Laverty had spotted during a plane ride.

What they found was Grajagan, or "G-Land," truly the exotic nirvana they set out to discover: a massive, mile-long coral reef that curves around to meet unmolested swells and bend them into racetrack walls with dreamy, top-to-bottom tubes. Finding the fantastic break was only the beginning, though; Boyum's brother returned soon thereafter and built the world's first surf camp, at the edge of the thick jungle, forever changing the way surfers could travel.

Surf Java

Location:
Indian Ocean
Country:
Indonesia
Language:
Multiple, including English
Currency:
Indonesian Rupiah

The Good . . .
- Warm water
- World-class surf
- Cheap

And the Bad . . .
- Winds
- Difficult access
- Malaria
- Sharks
- Shallow reef

Key to map
- Panaitan Rights, or Apocalypse
- Napalms
- Pussies
- One Palm Point
- Cimaja Beach
- Ombak Tujuh
- Turtles
- Grajagan

Left One of the world's best lefthanders, Grajagan.

Right South African professional Gavin Roberts extends his bottom turn on a solid wave at G-Land, setting up for the heavy tube section ahead.

Bali

Nusa Dua, Padang Padang, Uluwatu

Bali was the site of surfing's first forays into Indonesia and served as a launching pad for subsequent innumerable wave-hunting missions through the world's largest archipelago. A mysterious, almost mythical place when first surfed in the late 1960s and early '70s, Bali has since become a busy tourist hub, catering to the tens of thousands of surfers that drop in every year.

Bali has epic waves, water temperatures just above 80°F (27°C), prevailing offshore winds, and, for those interested in such activities, a hedonistic nightlife. Swells formed in the active South Indian Ocean are sent up nearly all year, peaking between April and October.

The Bukit Peninsula's east side is home to two ripping, right-hand reefs, Nusa Dua and Sanur, both of which are best during the rainy season, November into March. On the west side are Kuta Beach and Kuta Reef, a couple of popular city breaks, with reefs like Balangan, Dreamland, and Bingin farther south. On the western tip of the Bukit, though, are the main Bali draws, Padang Padang and Uluwatu.

Padang Padang, a wave so good they named it twice, is a flawless, top-speed, left-hand barrel ride running over slab reef and wrapping to a near-90-degree turn. Once dubbed the Balinese Pipeline, it needs a sufficient swell to work, but when the conditions are perfect so is Padang Padang. Just around the corner is Uluwatu, its bigger brother. A legendary left, first debuted in the 1972 film *Morning of the Earth*, Uluwatu immediately became an icon of exotic surf discovery, and the wave is definitely worthy of praise.

Starting at the outside section on a big day, the ride begins with a long drop as a huge, lefthand, high-speed wall and tubing shallow spots navigate into the Peak. It ends with a dip through the inside of the wave's blurry-fast, warping barrels along the Racetrack section. Although it is not as empty as it was in the '70s, Uluwatu generally spreads the crowd into a few different lineups with average-sized surf, and quickly filters out the pretenders when things get serious.

Above A calm day at a resort on Sanur Beach, enhanced by the scent of frangipani.

Surf Bali

Location:
Indian Ocean

Country:
Indonesia

Language:
Multiple, including English

Currency:
Indonesian Rupiah

The Good . . .
- Excellent waves
- Exotic locale
- Cheap

And the Bad . . .
- Crowds
- Shallow reef
- Motorcycles

Right Balinese standout Rizal Tanjung casually draws a line inside a picture-perfect barrel at Padang Padang: a wave so good they named it twice.

Key to map
- Sanur
- Nusa Dua
- Kuta Beach
- Kuta Reef
- Balangan
- Dreamland
- Bingin
- Padang Padang
- Uluwatu

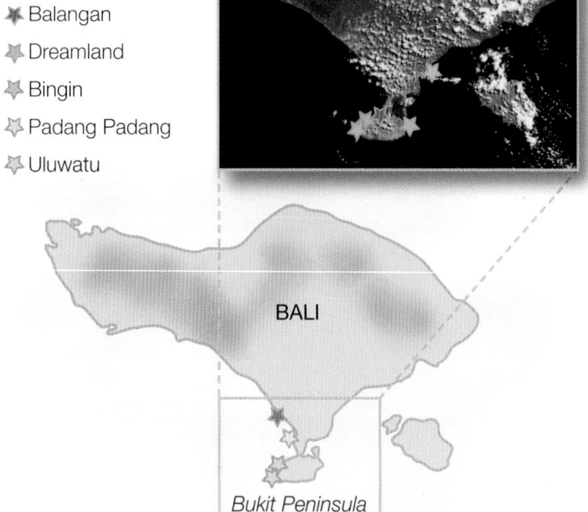

Lombok

Belongas, Ekas, Desert Point

Despite the fact that the Indonesian island of Lombok is only approximately twenty miles (32 km) across the channel from Bali, the pair seem hemispheres apart. Bali is densely tropical, and Lombok is dusty and arid; Bali is a bustling tourist center, and Lombok is slow paced and without luxury accommodations; Bali is blessed with a bevy of great surf breaks, and Lombok has just one awesome spot, the dreamy Desert Point, and a bunch of above-average waves.

Like the rest of the archipelago, consistent south and southwest swells from the "Roaring Forties" are the principal wave-making force, and offshore trade winds blow regularly. This pattern provides Lombok's south shore with plenty of waves, and the coast is filled with all kinds of surf: lefts and rights at Belongas and Mawun; small, barreling rights at Mawi; a variety of setups at Grupuk; and fast, grinding rights near Outside and Inside Ekas and Sereweh.

But even in this region of superlative surf, everything near or far pales in comparison to Desert Point on a big swell and favorable tide. Once dubbed the planet's best wave by a popular Australian surf magazine, Desert Point is one of the fastest, longest, and hollowest left barrels anywhere. With a habit of growing in size and speed as it moves down the shallow reef, Desert Point dares confident surfers to lock into its luscious caverns, offering promises of blurred, mind-melting tube rides to those bold enough to step inside.

Left Desert Point, superlative and enchanting, yet unbelievably shallow, sharp, and dangerous.

Right A receding tide backs off the sand at Tampa, just one of Lombok's many idyllic beaches.

Surf Lombok

Location:
Indian Ocean

Country:
Indonesia

Language:
Multiple, including English

Currency:
Indonesian Rupiah

The Good . . .

- Cheap
- One of the world's best waves

And the Bad . . .

- Lack of wave variety
- Shallow reef
- Rip currents
- Theft
- Malaria
- Crowds

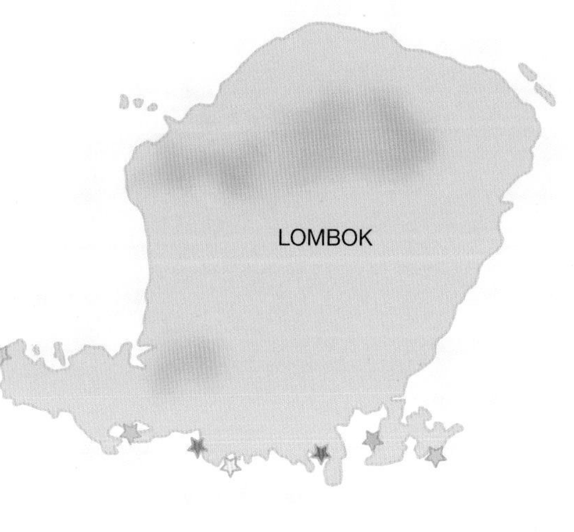

Key to map

- Desert Point
- Belongas
- Mawi
- Mawun
- Grupuk
- Outside/Inside Ekas
- Sereweh

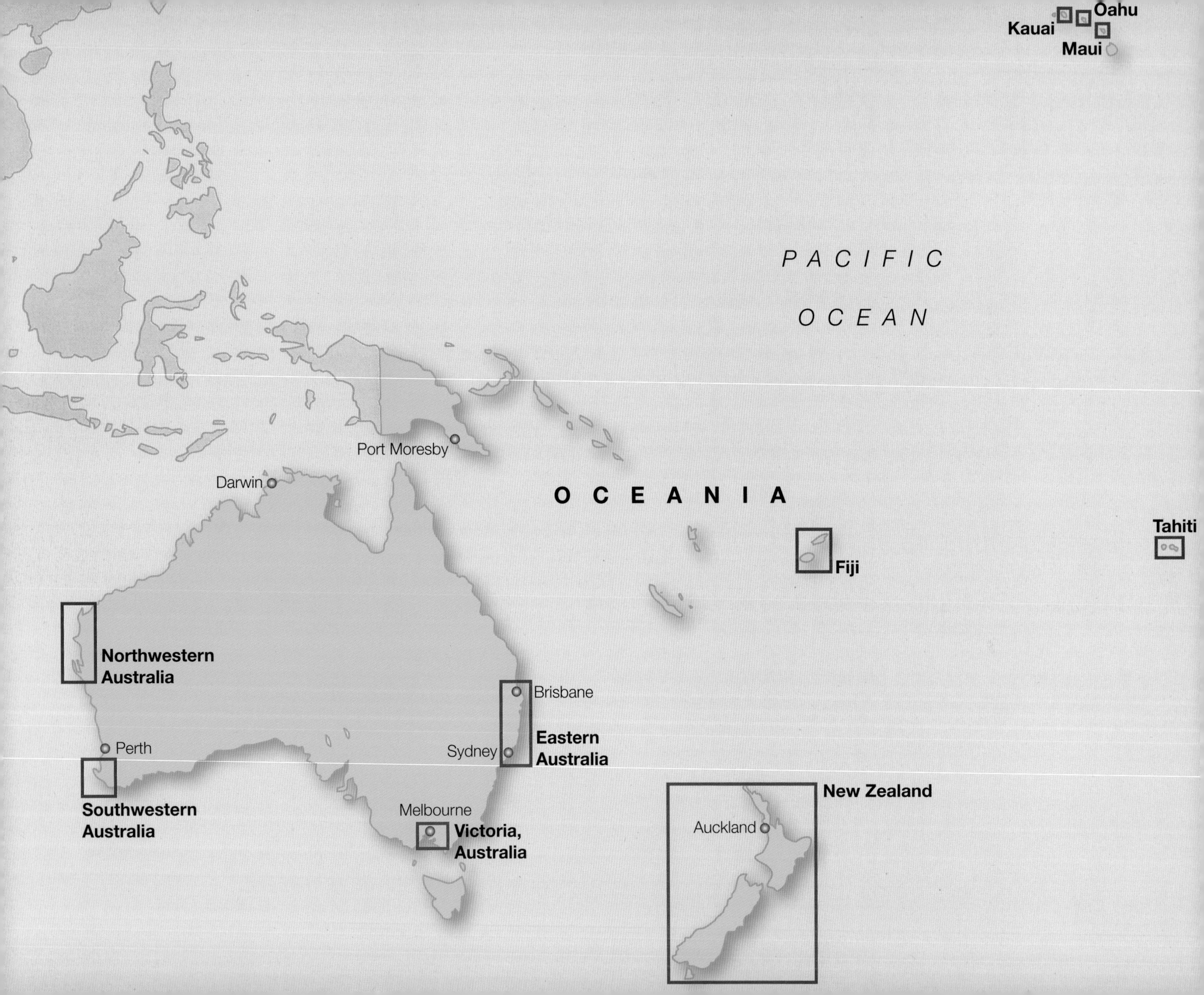

Oahu
Kauai
Maui
PACIFIC
OCEAN
Port Moresby
Darwin
OCEANIA
Tahiti
Fiji
Northwestern Australia
Brisbane
Eastern Australia
Sydney
Perth
Southwestern Australia
New Zealand
Melbourne
Victoria, Australia
Auckland

Oceania

The cradle of surf culture, Oceania is one of the Earth's most popular surf zones. The area covers thousands of square miles across two hemispheres and reaches into several time zones. It encompasses Australia to the west, the Hawaiian Islands to the north, New Zealand to the south, and Polynesian chains, including Tuamotu and Fiji, in the middle. The topography ranges from tropical island paradises in French Polynesia to deserts in Western Australia, and from active volcanoes in Hawaii to snow-covered mountain peaks in New Zealand.

The waves in this region are as diverse as its glorious island locales. Powerful reef passes, idyllic cobblestone point breaks, peaky beach breaks, offshore island retreats, even fierce, big-wave slabs—there is something on offer for every surfer, and of any skill level. The region is home to millions of local surfers and visited by hundreds of thousands of others every year.

The roots of modern surf culture are planted in Oceania, particularly in Hawaii. The easygoing lifestyle of the Waikiki beachboys, initially characterized by the spirit of *aloha*, surf trunks, flowery button-up shirts, and ukulele music, became adopted by visitors to Oahu in the early 1900s. Since then it has evolved into a global phenomenon. Much of the slang that is spoken by surfers worldwide today is compiled of words borrowed from the Hawaiian language mixed with witty Australian vernacular.

While on land and at sea, there are a few things of which the visitor should be aware. Across the region sharp, shallow reefs are one of the biggest hazards while surfing, and, as always, polluted ocean water poses a risk. Sharks, including the ferocious tiger shark and great white shark, roam throughout Oceania, and, when they patrol inshore areas, they are extremely dangerous, especially in murky conditions. Watch out for poisonous snakes, spiders, and insects. Always treat local surfers with respect. There are great times to be enjoyed here, whether you are visiting for the awesome waves, to soak up history, to relax on a beach with a view to a suntan and a drink, or to do all three.

Kauai

Prince Kuhio Park, Pakalas, Hanalei Point

Surfing on Kauai, one of Hawaii's outer islands, is generally reserved for serious practitioners. This tiny gem is raw, natural, and dangerous. It will take your breath away whether you are admiring the lush scenery from afar or pulling into a meaty barrel. Most of Kauai's best surf is powerful and hard to reach, but scoring some of these waves in all their glory will inspire animated tales and ensure your return to the Garden Isle.

Poipu, on the south shore, is Kauai's major tourist hub. This side of the island has a lively summer surf scene between May and October when southerly swells and northerly winds awaken several worthwhile waves. Besides a bevy of beachy spots, there are three breaks at Prince Kuhio Park that must be considered: PKs, also known as Longhouse, Centers, and Acid Drop.

The two most impressive breaks at Kauai, though, are Pakalas and Hanalei Point. Pakalas, or "Infinities," on the west side, is a long, fast, often hollow, hot-dogging left-hander that works with any south swell from three feet (1 m) to ten feet (3 m) and is seasonally groomed by tradewinds. A wave at Pakalas can line up for 300 yards (270 m) or more with several barrel sections when all three peaks connect.

Tucked into its namesake bay sits Hanalei Point, a magnet for the uninterrupted winter swells that originate in the Aleutian Islands and slam into the north side. Hanalei is one of the best rights in all of Hawaii. On calmer days, when wave heights range from three to six feet (1–2 m), Flat Rock and the Bowl, especially, provide welcoming, warm-water tubes and rippable shoulders. On premier days, Hanalei links its three sections, from Impossibles across Flat Rock and through the Bowl, with a series of sickening barrels and racetrack walls. When it is pumping like this, though, it's smart for all but the best surfers to take in the scene from the cliffs at Princeville, binoculars and mai tai in hand.

Right Talented East Side boy Elliot Leon, locked into a watery cavern on Kauai's North Shore.

Below Sea-level scenic of a Poipu sand strip.

Surf Kauai

Location:
Pacific Ocean

Country:
United States of America

Language:
English and Hawaiian

Currency:
US Dollar

The Good . . .
- Barrels
- Beautiful scenery
- Warm water
- Tropical climate

And the Bad . . .
- Rip currents
- Sharp reef and coral heads
- Tiger sharks
- Expensive

Key to map
- Hanalei Point
- Pakalas
- Acid Drop
- Centers
- Prince Kuhio Park

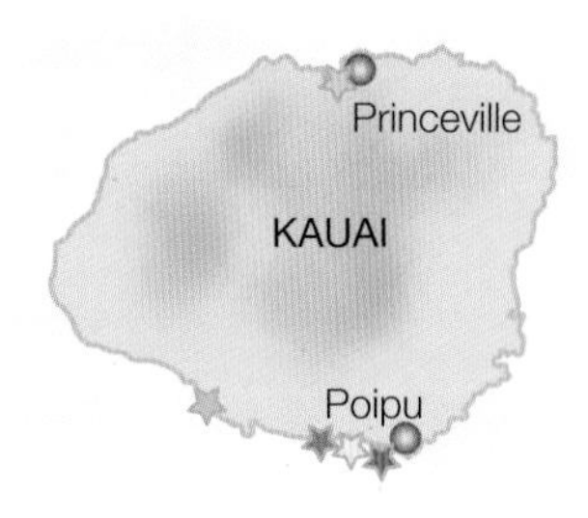

Oahu, North Shore

Haleiwa, Sunset Beach, Velzyland, Pipeline

The north shore of Oahu is the undisputed king of surf destinations. A popular haunt for thousands of hungry wave riders and photographers from October through March, the Seven Mile Miracle is the ultimate proving ground and can make or break any potential professional career. Nowhere on Earth is there a higher density of world-class breaks within such a short distance.

Some of the North Shore breaks were initially surfed in the 1920s and '30s, with tales of ancient Hawaiian royalty even testing the waters centuries ago. Word of this unique wave garden quickly spread beyond the tropical island chain and by the 1960s, the North Shore had become the dream destination for any surfer worth his or her mettle.

Situated many thousands of miles west of the United States mainland, smack dab in the North Pacific Ocean, the north side of Oahu is wide open to the west and northerly swells that roll in and smash into the isle, unimpeded by a continental shelf or barrier islands. Most spots close to the shore top out near fifteen feet (4.5 m), with Waimea Bay reaching twenty or more feet (6 m) and outer big-wave reefs occasionally reaching the forty-foot (12 m) range.

More than twenty named reef breaks fit into the seven-mile (11 km) stretch from Waiale'e down to Haleiwa, including some of the most famous spots in surfing. At Haleiwa is a namesake wave that hosts several contests each year on its shifty, high-performance rights and lefts, with fierce currents and a heaving inside section known as the Toilet Bowl.

At the far north end of the North Shore is Velzyland, a beautiful strip of shallow reef that creates some seriously hollow rights. V-land was once a spot wholly dominated by locals and avoided by outsiders. Nowadays, although still somewhat territorial, V-land is more often overrun with local and international bodyboarders.

To the south is Sunset Beach, probably ridden by the ancients and now one of the biggest names on the North Shore. This sectioning, sometimes well-shaped, moody

Surf Oahu, North Shore

Location:
Pacific Ocean

Country:
United States of America

Language:
English and Hawaiian

Currency:
US Dollar

The Good . . .
- World-class waves
- Warm water
- Photo possibilities

And the Bad . . .
- Crowds
- Sharp reefs
- Rip currents

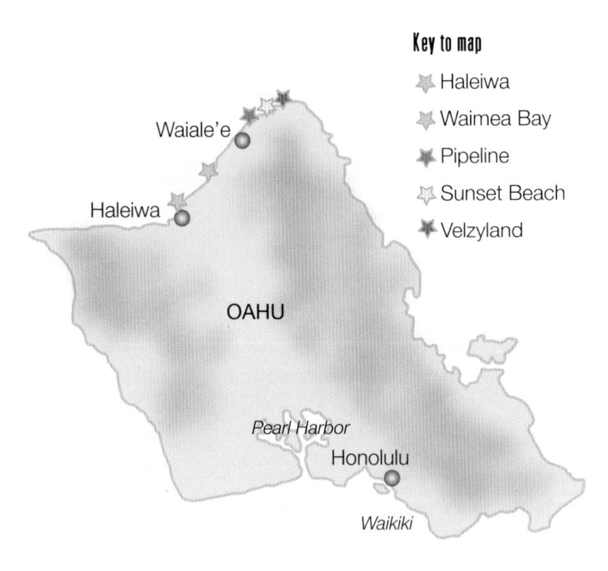

Right A tight set of waves rolls toward the reefs at the famous Pipeline, signaling the start of a strong swell.

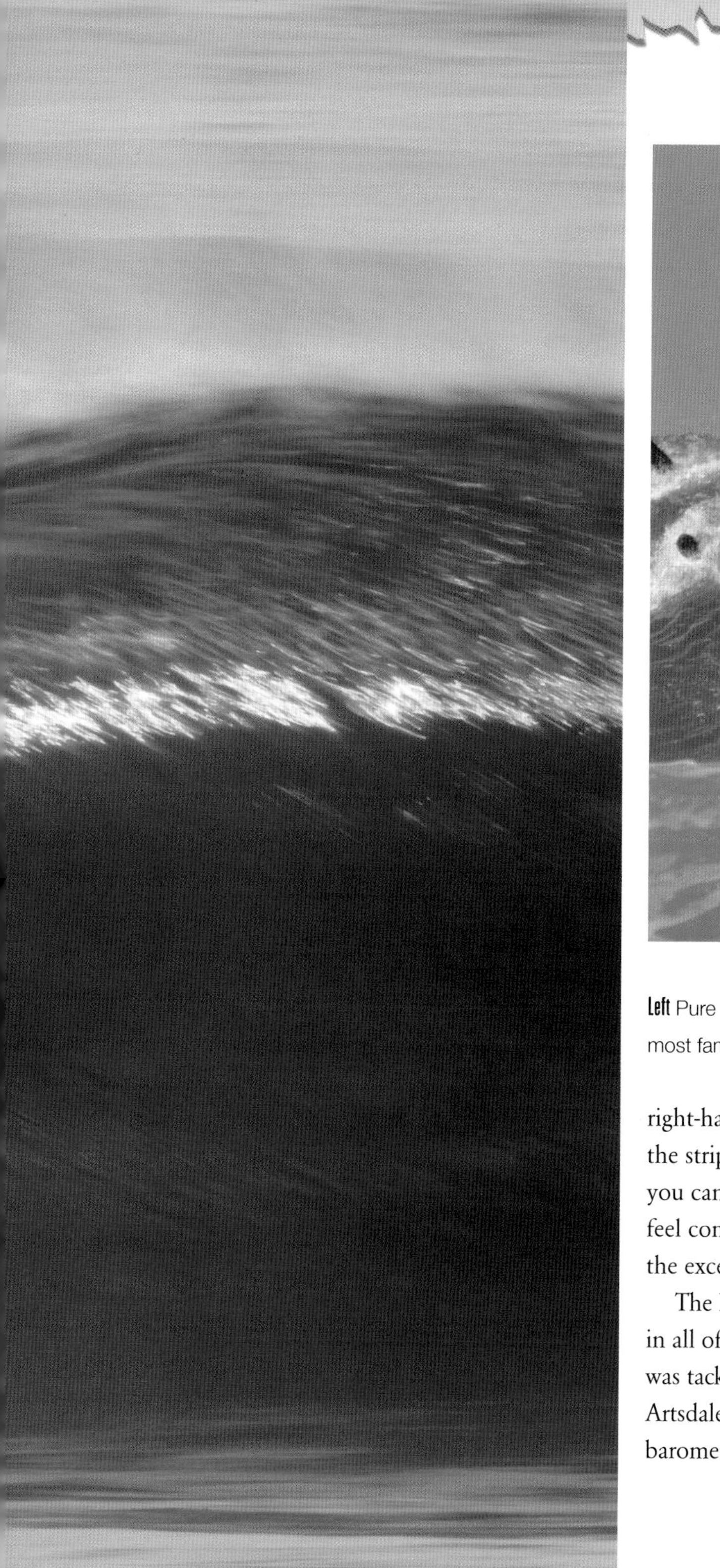

Left Pure cylindrical high-speed pleasure at The Pipe, home to the most famous barrels on Earth.

Above A more playful day at Pipeline, packed with the winter horde of surfers.

right-hander handles some of the largest in-shore surf on the strip and molds it into thick barrels and racy walls. If you can shine on a big day at Sunset, it is likely you will feel comfortable surfing nearly anywhere in Hawaii–with the exception of the Pipeline.

The Pipeline is positively the most-well-known name in all of surfing. Considered unrideable until the wave was tackled by Phil Edwards in 1961, and Butch Van Artsdalen and John Peck soon thereafter, Pipe is the barometer against which all other barreling waves in the world are measured. An insanely shallow, brutal reef break that sits very close to shore, the left-hand tubes found here are some of the most perfect and most photographed on the planet; getting photographed inside a Pipe pit might just land you inside one of the world's surf magazines. But don't think just showing up and paddling out will allow you to bask in Pipeline's barreling glory–the lineup here is intensely crowded, very skilled, and very local, and it has a decades-old pecking order that must be followed, unless you like asking for trouble.

Surf trunks

It was in the 1940s that today's surf style began to take shape, with surfers discarding their woolen two-piece suits for bare chests and narrow-waisted shorts called "trunks." A group from the Manhattan Beach Surf Club, including Dale Velzy and Barney Briggs, held a contest in which each had to wear a pair of white sailor pants, cut off just above the knees, for as long as possible without washing them. Reportedly, Velzy won the bet by keeping his on for three weeks. In the process, they found that the longer pants' legs prevented chafing on the surfers' thighs and, ever since, the long, baggy trunk has been the surfwear of choice, almost without a break.

MADE TO MEASURE

Some of the earliest custom-made surf trunks were found in Hawaii in the early 1950s. M. Nii, a tailor on Oahu, designed, sewed, and customized new shorts and trunks, as well as mending rips for the local surfers and visiting Californians and Aussies. In what most recognize as the first true surf trunk, known as M. Nii's "Makaha Drowner," sturdy, often double-seamed material was used, outfitted with drawstring ties and, eventually, a small, buttoned pocket for carrying a bar of paraffin surf wax or a wallet. M. Nii's trunks quickly became a way to distinguish the real surfers from the wannabes.

Back on the U.S. mainland, no commercial trunks of the same quality existed. Instead, surfers looked to their mothers to stitch a pair of trunks to replace their cutoff jeans while riding waves. The most famous of these sew-savvy women was Nancy Katin, who, with her husband, Walt, owned a small business that made industrial canvas boat covers in Surfside. As the story goes, local hot-dog surfer Corky Carroll asked Nancy to make him a pair of red trunks out of the tough canvas;

Opposite page The surfboards and bathing suits may have changed, but the attitude remains the same. A mid-1990s beach masquerade, with loose surf trunks and skimpy bikinis (top); and the short and long of surf trunk–style as it was in 1960s Malibu (bottom).

This page, clockwise from left These days, it only takes a board and a pair of baggy board shorts to pose as a surfer; the pros of the mid-'60s Hang Ten surf team were surf legends like Bing Copeland, Phil Edwards, Greg Noll, and Nat Young; a classic example of vintage, sturdy surf trunks.

she obliged, using the same, strong stitches and indestructible thread as the boat covers received. Carroll's new trunks drew the collective attention of the neighborhood surfers, and it wasn't long before Nancy was filling trunk orders by the thousands. She eventually turned the family boat-cover company into a thriving surf trunk business they called Kanvas by Katin.

NEW MATERIALS FOR OLD STYLES

Other surf trunk companies arose in the 1960s, such as Birdwell Beach Britches, Hang Ten, and Ocean Pacific (OP). Hang Ten and OP saw a chance to capitalize on the growing "coolness" of the sport, and pitched their clothes at the mainstream youth market. Once their garments hit the big chain stores, though, the two lines were snubbed by core surfers. The two decades that followed witnessed a global boom in surf wear. In the mid-1970s, Quiksilver, based in Australia, rode the popularity of their Velcro-fly, high-legged trunks, which they called "board shorts," immediately becoming a major player and making Velcro a lasting surf-trunk staple. More surf lines, like Australia's Billabong and California's Maui and Sons, joined the new wave in the 1980s, when trunks regressed into bright-colored, short-cut styles for about ten years.

Today, the surf trunk market is overflowing with new and old companies producing slight twists on the same theme with each new season. Big companies like O'Neill, Hurley, Patagonia, Volcom, Rip Curl, and Rusty, along with smaller ones such as Oxbow, RVCA, Da Hui, and Matix, compete against industry giants Quiksilver and Billabong for a piece of the multibillion dollar surf-wear pie. Trunks, now known as board shorts, have returned to the long-legged, single-pocket design established so long ago, but are these days built of high-tech materials that dry quickly, stretch, prevent rashes, or come from greener alternatives like recycled plastic or polyester.

Oahu, South Shore

Queens, Number Threes, Ala Moana

Waikiki, on the south shore of Oahu, is undisputedly one of the most famous stretches of beach in the surfing world. The earliest romantic black-and-white images of Hawaiian wave riders on heavy, solid-wood plank *alaia* and *olo* cruising across the sloping, gentle waves in kinglike stances were taken here. It is said that the beach at Waikiki, now often referred to as "Town," was a favorite gathering place for the ancient surfers, too, with some breaks reserved strictly for island royalty.

The waves and beach scene at Waikiki remained the face of surfing well into the mid-twentieth century, with more than a dozen prime peaks and several lesser, yet still high-quality, spots. To this day, Town remains at the top of any real surfer's must-see list–feeling the frangipani-scented trade winds blowing over the Duke Kahanamoku statue and into the warm, powder-blue waves is an experience not likely forgotten.

Beyond the current hustle and bustle of city life, the surf is still the main attraction. Best just before, after, and during summer, when south swells move up from the South Pacific, popular spots like Number Threes and Queens–a fast, bowly, hot-dog wave that spins over shallow reef–get crowded with longboarders, short-boarders, stand-up paddle surfers, and even outrigger canoes. The jewel of Town, though, is Ala Moana. Known to most as "Bowls," the wave was created in 1952 when the Ala Wai Harbor entrance was built. A steep, round, barreling left, Ala Moana has been a haven for high-performance South Shore surfers from Sam Lee, sometimes noted as the world's first real tube-riding specialist, to Gerry Lopez, the world's most famous tube rider, to the current crop of respected locals.

Surf Oahu, South Shore

Location:
Pacific Ocean

Country:
United States of America

Language:
English and Hawaiian

Currency:
US Dollar

The Good . . .
- Birthplace of modern surfing
- Trade winds
- Warm water

And the Bad . . .
- Crowds
- Speeding cars
- Sharp reefs
- Expensive

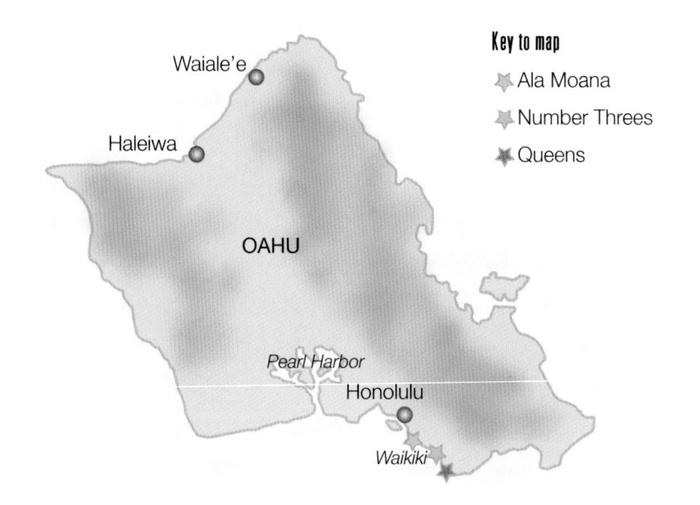

Below An incredible Waikiki sunset ends a classic day at Queens. Soaking up the South Shore scene is an experience to treasure.

Right Oahu local Sean Moody sets up for a barrel ride at Ala Moana. Summertime means south swells and surfing "Town."

Maui

Kanaha, Jaws, Ma'alaea, Honolua Bay

The second-largest island in the Hawaiian chain, Maui has been a top draw for traveling surfers and tourists alike since the 1950s. There is little reason to wonder why this wondrously beautiful place is such a popular destination. Maui is home to a handful of famous waves–such as Honolua Bay, Ma'alaea, and Jaws–despite many swells being shadowed by Molokai, Lanai, and the Big Island, Hawaii. Because of their shelter, Maui's swell windows are limited, so it is difficult for the island to receive much from the northwest, west, and southeast, but it does well with what it gets. The Valley Isle is also well known for its world-class windsurfing and kite-boarding conditions, but the strong cross-shore winds often ruin some good days for prone surfers.

Some great waves are located on Maui's north coast; unfortunately, this part of the island gets extremely windy early on most days. Close to Kahului, Kanaha can produce classic, right-hand point-break waves. The Harbor at Kahului is powerful and fun, but it is known for its shark-filled waters. There is a run of other reefs from Kanaha to Hookipa that turn on, plus the outer reef big wave outside Spreckelsville, a jaw-dropping sight. Off the northeast corner of Maui lives Jaws, one of the world's biggest waves–known also as "Peahi." When Jaws is large and working, only a select few tow in, and the rest watch from the surrounding bluffs.

In northwestern Maui you can find a lot of wave activity near Lahaina when south and northeast swells sneak in. In town there is the Harbor, a jacking, vertical peak tailor made for cutting-edge surfing, and probably forty other spots within a few miles. One of the best is Ma'alaea, south of town, a fickle but outstanding streamline barrel with prevailing offshore winds, known as the fastest rideable wave on Earth. The other is Honolua Bay, a gorgeous right often considered the symbol of perfect surf, for regular-footers at least. Honolua is a top-to-bottom, point-style wave with high-performance walls and several tube sections set in an idyllic bay. A good day at Honolua Bay is what dreams are made of.

Surf Maui

Location:
Pacific Ocean

Country:
United States of America

Language:
English and Hawaiian

Currency:
US Dollar

The Good . . .
- World-class waves
- Warm water
- Ideal scenery

And the Bad . . .
- Sharks
- Wind
- Crowds

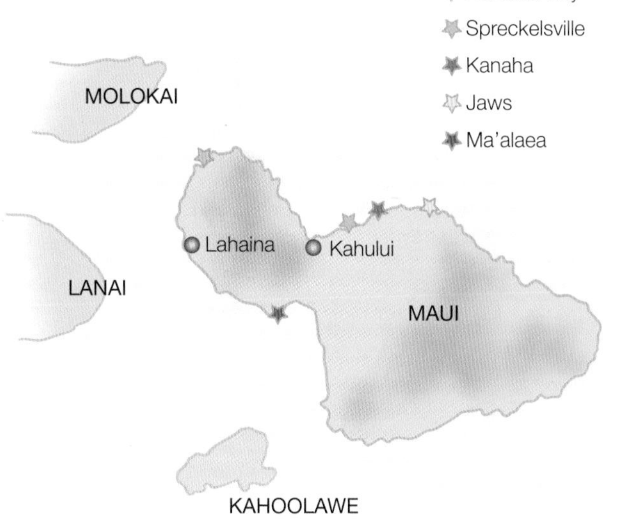

Left The stout, inside section at Honolua Bay opens up to say "Aloha."

Right Scoring an epic ride at Honolua is definitely fodder for the mind-bank scrapbook.

"Things that, previously, they only dreamed of . . . suddenly these surfers were doing it!"

—Sam George, in *Riding Giants*

Charging Peahi

Better known to surfers as "Jaws," Peahi is a monumental wave that awakens a handful of times each year. Jaws was first ridden in the late 1980s by some of Maui's finest windsurfers, including Dave Kalama, Rush Randle, and Mike Waltze. However, it would take a few years before the intimidating reef break became known to the masses.

Towing into big waves started, most agree, in 1992, when Darrick Doerner, Laird Hamilton, and Buzzy Kerbox used an inflatable dinghy with an outboard engine, a water-ski rope, and long pintail guns to harness the board speed necessary to catch monster surf on Oahu's North Shore. The following year, sights were set on Maui, the rubber boat traded for more maneuverable personal watercraft, and boards tailored specifically for tow-in surfing. The subsequent assaults on Jaws produced staggering images of thirty- to forty-foot (9–12 m) waves, ridden by legends like Hamilton and Kalama.

Now, whenever reports forecast massive swells at Jaws, tow-in crews, photographers, and helicopter movie cameramen descend upon Maui, while spectators line the cliffs for a glimpse of the death-defying action.

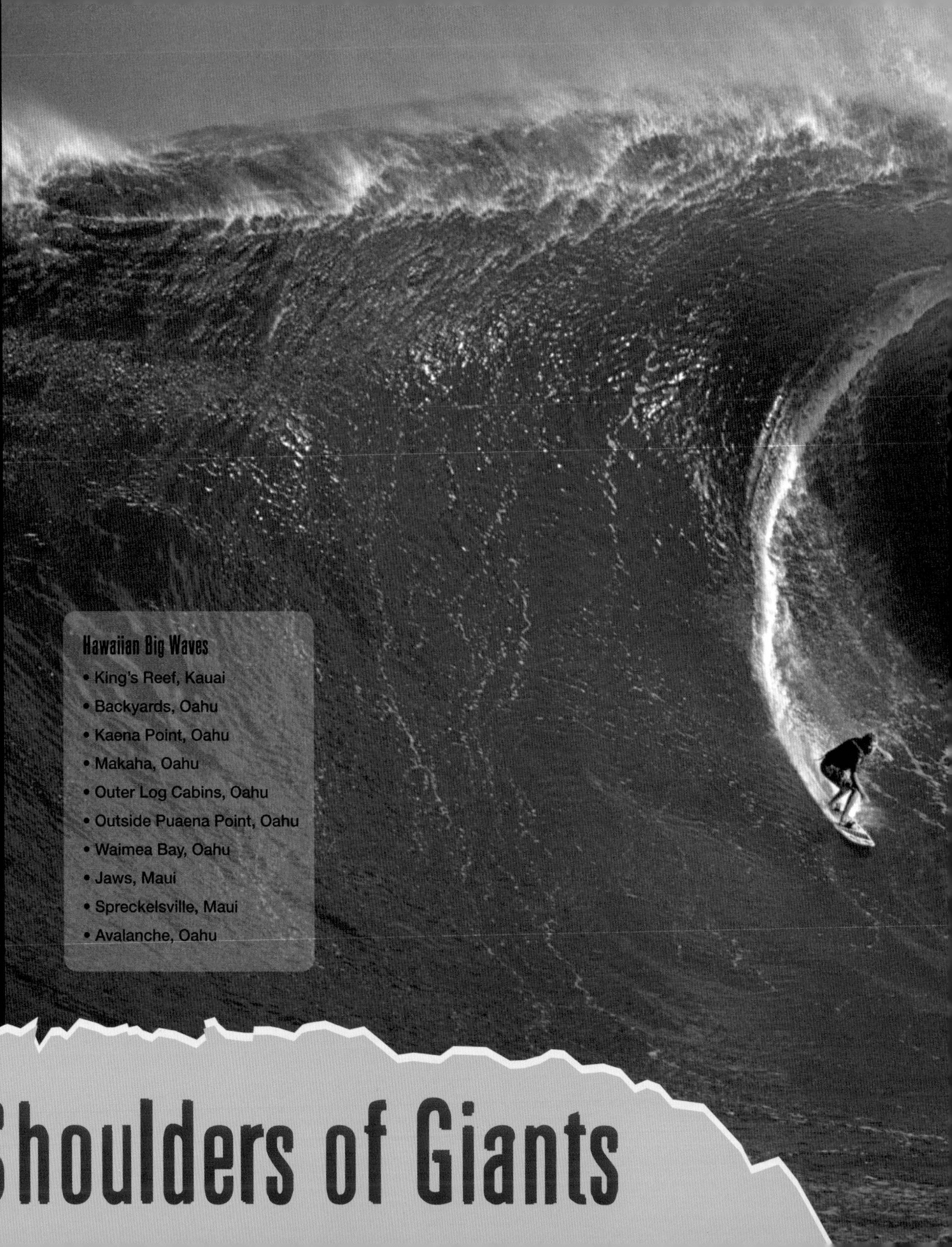

Hawaiian Big Waves

- King's Reef, Kauai
- Backyards, Oahu
- Kaena Point, Oahu
- Makaha, Oahu
- Outer Log Cabins, Oahu
- Outside Puaena Point, Oahu
- Waimea Bay, Oahu
- Jaws, Maui
- Spreckelsville, Maui
- Avalanche, Oahu

Riding on the Shoulders of Giants

Hawaii's first big waves

Hawaii has always been a mecca for big waves. One of the first big waves explored in Hawaii was Waikiki's Outside Castles—a rare, outer-reef left made famous by the legendarily long rides Duke Kahanamoku is said to have completed there. As the focus of surfing on Oahu shifted away from the South Shore and toward bigger, more powerful waves in the 1930s, local surfers like Wally Froiseth, John Kelly, and Fran Heath began paddling into ten-foot-plus point surf at the West Side break of Makaha on their chopped-down "hot curls" (one of the earliest big-wave surfboard design improvements). In 1953, a photo of perfectly big Makaha being ridden by Buzzy Trent, George Downing, and Woody Brown first appeared in a California newspaper, basically solidifying the island's place in big-wave lore. In 1969, thirty-five-foot (10 m) surf at Makaha was tackled by the inimitable Greg "Da Bull" Noll; it was easily the biggest wave surfed up to that point.

By then, though, Makaha's spot as top big-wave dog had been overtaken by Waimea Bay, when, in 1957, a group of Californian surfers led by the Noll charged into twenty-footers at the sacred, taboo spot. Waimea, found on the North Shore, accommodates Oahu's biggest winter swells and molds them into jacking right-handers, daring paddle-in surfers to drop in and safely outrun the mountains of whitewater chasing after them. The big-wave game has changed a lot during the past fifty years, but Waimea Bay remains a world-famous destination for paddling into giant surf.

Left Young Hawaiian waterman Mark Healey escapes the potentially lethal clutches of a towering wave on a heart-pumping day at Jaws.

Northwestern Australia

Jake's, Red Bluff, Gnaraloo

Western Australia's northwestern region, ranging from Geraldton up to Exmouth, is a harsh, dry desert. A rugged stretch of coastline that requires traveling surfers to pack everything they might need for the entire trip into a reliable four-wheel-drive vehicle, this part of Australia is raw and mostly unpopulated. Hardy visitors can reap the area's rewards with a strong will, courage, a helmet, and a pintail gun to protect against injuries from dangerous waves and shallow reefs.

Its proximity to the Roaring Forties' powerful wave-making capabilities sends strong, short-fetch swells into Western Australia for most of the year. These remain at four feet (1.3 m) to eight feet (2.4 m) throughout the year and are biggest between April and September, with waves up to fifteen feet (5 m) possible. Western Australia is the only state in the entire country to receive the same swells that eventually light up Indonesia, only they make landfall here, at the country's most northwesterly point, faster, bigger, and in a less-organized fashion.

There are a few fierce waves in and around Geraldton, such as Hell's Gate and Drummonds, but farther north is where most of the attention is drawn. Near Kalbarri is where you can find Jake's, a picturesque left with a very steep takeoff zone over reef with shoulders that throw out intense barrels.

The beautiful left-hand tube at Red Bluff can be found about sixty miles (95 km) north of Carnavon. A long, fast wave requiring a long paddle, the Bluff rips down the point and opens up perfect, ruler-edge tubes for those lucky souls who find themselves there at the right time. Red Bluff may be an iconic spot but about an hour north is Gnaraloo, a wave that gets as crazy as its name sounds. Gnaraloo is another sharky and shallow left with high-performance walls and a propensity to produce mutant, jacking barrels, especially when it reaches double-overhead or bigger. It is also a very long way from anywhere and far from any medical facilities.

Surf Northwestern Australia

Location:
Indian Ocean

Country:
Australia

Language:
English and native languages

Currency:
Australian Dollar

The Good . . .
- Powerful waves
- Smaller crowds than in most of Australia

And the Bad . . .
- Sharks
- Shallow reef
- Cold water

Right The impressive peak known as Noisys is just one reason this part of Australia lures so many surfers.

Southwestern Australia

The Box, The Point/Margaret River

The southwestern tip of the country accepts the same massive Indian Ocean swells as the rest of Western Australia, in addition to some action from the Southern Ocean. However, most of the similarities with the state's desert region farther north end there, for this area is much more temperate, greener, and bound by vineyard-lined hills and endemic eucalyptus forests.

This concentrated stretch of surfing locales, from Cape Naturaliste to Cape Leeuwin, is extremely consistent, too, with flat days being virtually nonexistent here. In fact, waves rarely drop below two feet (0.6 m), and they can also reach the twenty-foot (6 m) realm more than a few times during Australia's southern-hemisphere winter, from June to August. While the coast of southwestern Australia is filled with powerful breaks, some of the best are found outside the town of Margaret River. Off Cape Mentelle, The Box is more of a mutating rush of ocean than a wave, but it does create exciting air drops into square barrels over barely covered slab reef with big swells and high tides–perfect for those fearless surfers who want to have a go at this famous spot.

Margaret River's main wave at Surfer's Point–known simply as "The Point"–though, is the feature story here. Its waves are created by the flat limestone reef that juts out, with channels on each side. The Point produces freight-train-speed rights and lefts that are highlighted by big walls and heavy barrels, which can hold form at a serious size, triple-overhead or larger.

Surf Southwestern Australia

Location:
Indian Ocean and Southern Ocean

Country:
Australia

Language:
English and native languages

Currency:
Australian Dollar

The Good...
- Variety of great waves
- Consistent swells

And the Bad...
- Sharks
- Cold water
- Shallow reefs

Key to map
The Box
The Point/ Margaret River

Cape Naturaliste
Margaret River
Cape Leeuwin

Far left UK surfer Tom Doidge-Harrison charges through a blue cavern, just a few feet above the slab reef at The Box.

Left A crew of kiteboard surfers takes to the ocean on a small and breezy afternoon at Prevelly Beach, Margaret River.

Victoria, Australia

Flynn's Reef, Winkipop, Bell's Beach

Australia's southernmost state, Victoria, is renowned around the surfing world for a couple of things: hosting the country's longest-running professional surfing contest, at Bell's Beach, and being home to two of the biggest companies in the surfing industry, Rip Curl and Quiksilver. Obviously one of Australia's major surfing centers, the southeastern tip of Oz holds some all-time spots as well as the world's first surfing recreation reserve. Victoria, sitting on the ridge that demarcates the Tasman Sea and Southern Ocean, receives consistent swells all year, but it also receives the coldest weather in all of Australia. Surf gets biggest between April and October here, with heights anywhere from four feet (1.3 m) to double-overhead and beyond.

The geography of Victoria's Mornington Peninsula and Phillip Island makes for some of the state's most unique setups. Mornington spots such as Quarantines, Cape Shank, Meanos, Suicides, and Crunchies Point offer a variety of beginner- to expert-level waves, and west- and east-facing shores here enable surfers to find a wind-sheltered break by just taking a short drive; similarly, Phillip Island's favorite rights of Flynn's Reef and Summerland Bay, and the ledging barrels found at Express Point, among others, make this tiny island a mini wave wonderland.

One of the best things about southern Victoria is its easy coastal access and the beautiful views afforded by the Great Ocean Road, from Apollo Bay to Torquay. Beneath the two-lane highway are spread some of Victoria's most popular beaches, including Kennet River, Lorne, Cathedral Rock, and Point Roadnight. However, everything in Victoria is overshadowed by Winkipop and Bell's Beach, part of a national Surfing Recreation Reserve. Winkipop is a phenomenal wave, a lightning-fast right with walls that can stretch 300 yards (275 m), plus barrel sections aplenty, and it would be the region's main attraction were it not for its famous neighbor, Bell's Beach. A perfectly blank canvas for high-performance board strokes, the racy walls between the sections at Bell's are thick with drama and history. Getting a complete ride from Centreside through to The Bowl will make any mortal surfer feel like a champion.

Surf Victoria

Location:
Southern Ocean and Tasman Sea

Country:
Australia

Language:
English and native languages

Currency:
Australian Dollar

The Good . . .
- Consistent swells
- Beach access
- Amount of waves

And the Bad . . .
- Cold water
- Crowds
- Rip currents
- Winds
- Sharks

Key to map
- Bell's Beach
- Winkipop
- Quarantines
- Cape Shank
- Meanos
- Suicides
- Flynn's Reef
- Express Point

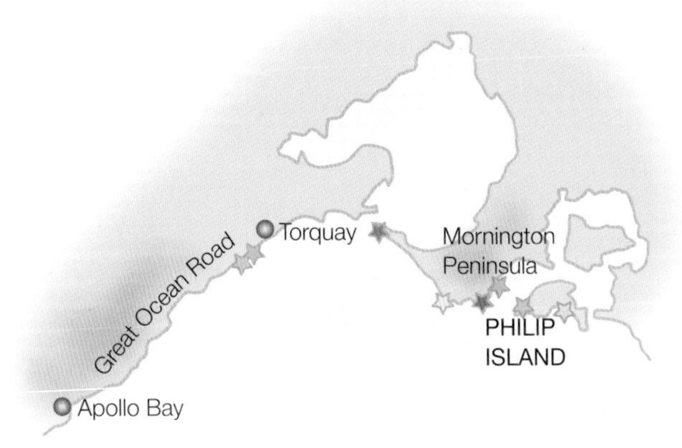

Left Flawless lines sweep in from the Southern Ocean—truly, this is Bell's Beach at its best.

Right "Part two" of Southern Victoria's dynamic wave duo, Winkipop.

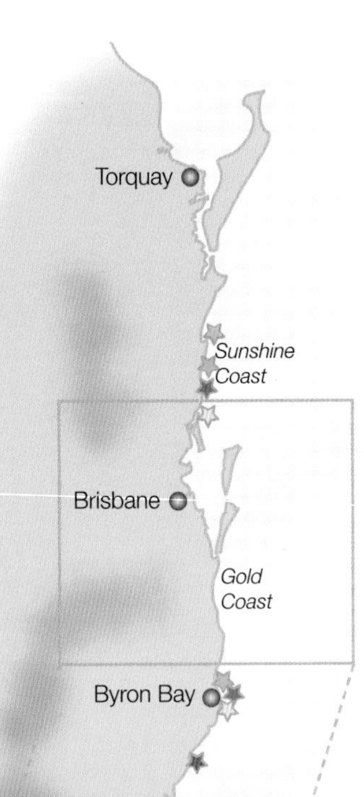

Eastern Australia

Lennox Head, The Pass, Kirra, Noosa Heads

Surf Eastern Australia

Location:
Pacific Ocean

Country:
Australia

Language:
English and native languages

Currency:
Australian Dollar

The Good . . .
- Historical coast
- Variety of surf
- Urban and natural settings
- World-class waves

And the Bad . . .
- Expensive
- Crowds
- Sharks
- Jellyfish

The east coast of Australia, broadly from Sydney north to Sandy Cape (on Fraser Island, facing Torquay), encompasses the wave-rich states of New South Wales (NSW) and Queensland. This is by far the most-visited stretch of the country, as well as being home to the greatest concentration of local surfers, and the scenery shifts between cityscape and rural landscapes. A region blessed with year-round waves ranging from two feet (0.6 m) to six feet (2 m), Australia's east coast offers something for every type of surfer to fall in love with.

The national surf capital, Sydney, offers large beach breaks such as Manly and Narrabeen. Freshwater Beach is known for hosting Duke Kahanamoku's 1914 surfing demonstration, a historic event that launched surfing in Australia. Other structured breaks in the area,

Local Stuart Cadden scores a shapely righthander at a secret spot in northern New South Wales.

including Fairy Bower's long rights at the headland and the top-to-bottom barrels of Dee Why Point, get classic when the southerly swells reach the four-foot (1.3 m) to five-foot (1.6 m) level.

One of New South Wales's other main surf areas, Byron Bay, lies hundreds of miles north and light-years away from the congested city life of Sydney. Much of Byron Bay is still an untouched, natural environment, popular with artists, hippies, and, of course, surfers looking to escape freeway traffic and the rat race. However, these days, it must be noted, even an enclave like this is slowly being built up. South of Byron is the country's unmatched point break of Lennox Head. Often compared to South Africa's Jeffrey's Bay for its pure speed, power, hollowness, and capability to handle sizeable wells, Lennox has remained at the lead of Australian surfboard testing grounds since the 1960s.

Back in Byron Bay proper, several spots circle the cape, such as Tallows, Wategoes, Clark's, and The Wreck, all requiring a decent east or northeast swell in order to happen, usually between November and April. Byron's best section, though, is The Pass, a lengthy wave with a rock and sandbar bottom that spins cylindrical barrels across some sections. The Pass fronts a picturesque point and is home to several pods of dolphins–truly a gorgeous place.

Just north of the NSW-Queensland border, around 50 miles (80 km) south of Brisbane, is Australia's most famous and most crowded region, the Gold Coast. Containing dreamy breaks like Duranbah, Snapper Rocks, Greenmount, Kirra, Currumbin, and Burleigh Heads, the waves on the Goldie are legendary, and, thus, extremely crowded. Kirra is one of the planet's best barrels, a mechanical tube that winds down the sandy point with speed and leaves legs cramped from crouching inside its hollow for so long. Whatever Kirra's waves lack in size, they surely make up for it with their sheer perfection. Such excellence lures crowds like bees to the flower, though, making Kirra possibly the most crowded break on Earth.

Below A classic look at Kirra doing its thing.

Those Queenslanders seeking to escape Kirra's madness often begin just north on the trail to Noosa Heads, into the Sunshine Coast. Here the crowds thin, although the natural fauna becomes more hazardous. The Sunshine's shore is deep in sandbar beach breaks between King's Beach, in Caloundia, and Alexandria Bay, in the north, with places like the Bluff, Point Cartwright, and Moffats offering right-point respite. But when the right amount of correctly angled swell turns on the Sunshine Coast, all roads lead to Noosa Heads, a fantastic series of five right-hand points lining the headland. From Granite Bay, to Ti Tree, National Park (also known as Noosa), Johnson's, and First Point, each point section offers something a little different from its neighbor. Mellow sections, sucking takeoff zones, spinning barrels, speedy walls, ruler-edge peelers, and size–all combine to create a regular-footer's watery amusement park.

Above The Pass at Byron Bay is a stunningly gorgeous spot where the waves get very good; but be sure to bring a battle ax and body armor to defend against the intense surf crowd.

New Zealand

Makarori Point, Tuamotu Island, Raglan

New Zealand is one of the most peaceful and scenic destinations on Earth. A pair of main islands lying a thousand miles off Australia's southeastern edge, New Zealand's interior is lush with vegetation and dense with mountains, deep valleys, and towering peaks that boast fantastic skiing and snowboarding conditions. The country's coastal regions are equally varied, with sweeping bays, plunging cliffs, and acres of farmland; both on the coast and inland, the terrain varies greatly from south to north. The ocean is clean, blue-green, and usually chilly enough to require a full rubber wettie.

Above Time for a lunch break and to dry the wetties in between go-outs at Gisborne's Pine Beach.

Left Dan Frodsam hopped on a short flight from his Australian homeland over to New Zealand for some Kiwi bowls at Raglan.

Surf New Zealand

Location:
Tasman Sea and South Pacific Ocean

Country:
New Zealand

Language:
English and Maori

Currency:
New Zealand Dollar

The Good . . .
- Variety of good waves
- Beautiful scenery
- Few crowds
- Friendly locals

And the Bad . . .
- Cold water
- Difficult wave access
- Occasional great white sharks

The indigenous Maori were seen riding waves on crude surfboards and canoes by explorers as far back as the 1600s and likely have been surfing for as long as they have been there. The missionaries who arrived toward the end of the nineteenth century all but ended Maori surfing, similar to what was happening to the Hawaiians around the same time. The sport's resurgence began in 1915, when Duke Kahanamoku demonstrated stand-up surfboard riding on the North Island.

Today, more than three-quarters of New Zealand's population lives on the North Island. The majority of named surf breaks are to be found here, too, and they include every type of wave setup imaginable. With the west coast bordering the Tasman Sea and the east coast set against the South Pacific Ocean–and the two located only a six-hour drive apart–the wave playground of New Zealand is unlike any other on Earth. Since the entire country is blessed with great surf, "best" is a relative term in New Zealand when considering the top wave zones.

New Zealand receives waves all year round and from all sides, with 360 degrees of swell window. Onshore winds can be an issue, but you can almost always find somewhere nearby that is more sheltered or head farther offshore.

The North Island's east coast is a very rich region indeed, and Gisborne is the surfing heart: Makarori Point is a long, right-hand reef break with continuous shoulders, popular with those who enjoy laying it on rail; Wainui Beach is a consistently high-performance reef and beach break with several peaks such as Whales, Pines, and Stock Route; and the sandbars at Gizzy Pipe occasionally suck up into dreamy tube rides. Gisborne's finest wave, though, is Tuamotu Island, a very hollow, long left that appears out of deep water and wraps around the small headland.

On the opposite side of the North Island, the west coast sees even more consistent surf with too many excellent waves to list here, especially in the Taranaki zone. But New Zealand's crown jewel and best-known spot is undoubtedly Raglan. Located west of the town of Hamilton, Raglan is a world-class, left point setup consisting of three main sections. Indicator, found farthest outside, is the least pressured, with waves that scream down the line with challenging barrels over the shallows. Whale Bay, the middle segment, enjoys a somewhat steadier pace with waves that are perfect for carving, cutting back, and smacking the lip. The inside stretch, called Manu, is a very fast lineup of sucking caverns and deep pits connecting past the river mouth. Legend has it that when big swells and low tides meet, the whole place can link together to form ridiculous, leg-numbing lefts that sprint across the entire point for nearly two miles.

Left Hypnotic, ruler-edge lines march toward the fabled points at Raglan. Since the area's worldwide debut in *The Endless Summer*, its long lefts have become legendary.

Below California stylist C. J. Nelson guides a fine noseride across one of New Zealand's lesser-known lefthand point breaks.

Fiji

Swimming Pools, Restaurants, Cloudbreak

Situated off the west coast of Viti Levu, the largest of Fiji's more than three hundred islands, are Tavarua and Namotu, two of the Mamanuca Islands. To most surfers, the all-inclusive resorts found on these islets represent the dream vacation: tropical weather; warm, crystalline water; local beer; fresh fish; and private, world-class outer reef waves accessible only by boat.

In the mid-1980s, when the phenomenal surf encircling this pair of tiny islands was first experienced, entrepreneurial surfers made deals to establish resorts on Tavarua and Namotu, including exclusive rights to the nearby reefs. The result was two expensive island getaways that offer–albeit with limited availability–the trip of a lifetime during the high surf season, between April and October.

On Namotu, an island so tiny that throwing a rock across it is not out of the question, one can reach the two right-hand breaks of Wilkes Pass, which delivers speeding, round tube rides, and Swimming Pools, a long, less-intimidating wave with clear-as-glass water. There is also Namotu Lefts, the most critical wave on Namotu, and the only left. If you fall you will likely get hurt, but if you surf it well you may be greatly rewarded.

Tavarua, though, is the bigger draw, with the lure of Restaurants, one of the longest and cleanest left-hand barrels on the planet. Expert surfers have been timed inside for a mind-numbing twenty-five seconds while screaming dangerously close to the sucking reef below their feet. But the spot that takes the cake is Cloudbreak, an awesome offshore reef wave that winds, grinds, and speeds through three distinct sections that can connect, on big swells, into one long and hollow thrill ride.

Surf Fiji

Location:
Pacific Ocean
Country:
Fiji
Language:
English, Fijian and Hindustani
Currency:
Fijian Dollar

The Good . . .
- World-class reef waves
- Exotic locale
- Friendly people

And the Bad . . .
- Expensive accommodations
- Shallow reef
- Sun exposure
- Limited access/availability

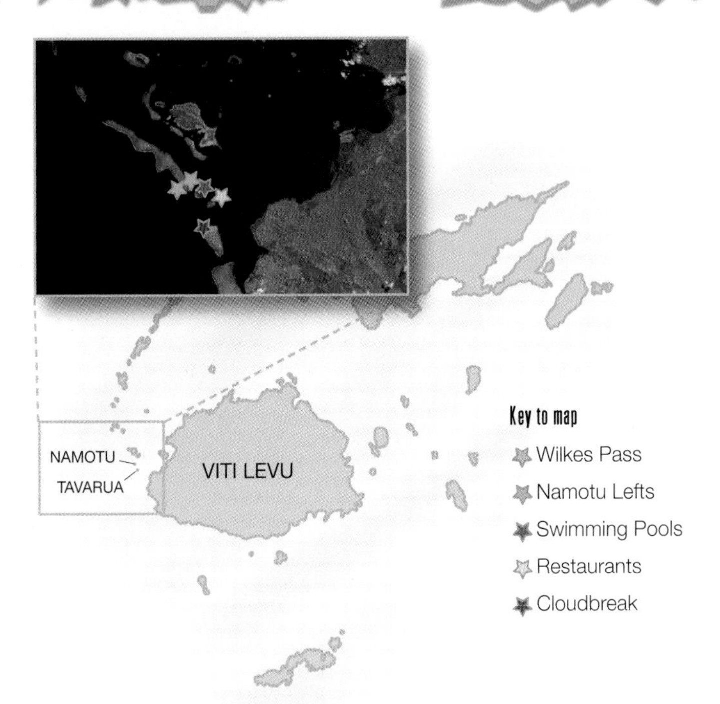

Above The minuscule Fijian island of Tavarua is blessed with a few of the most sought-after surf spots on the planet.

Right The ultra-shallow Shish Kabobs section at Cloudbreak, the epitome of a high-risk, high-reward wave.

Californian surfer Tyler Stanlan calmly cruises through a barrel on a small day at Teahupoo.

Tahiti

Matavai, Taapuna, Maraa, Vairao, Teahupoo

Surfing on the two tiny Tahitian islands is a tradition that goes back centuries. Although it is likely that surfing was practiced in Tahiti for much of the last thousand years, reports, documented by explorer Captain James Cook and his crew, first appeared in the late 1770s.

There are few places more stunning than Tahiti, in the chain of Society Islands. This idyllic tropical destination has verdant, rain-soaked mountains, which slope down to picturesque towns that dot the two circular-shaped coastlines. These are rimmed by white and black sand beaches that are in turn bordered by barrier reefs, a powder-blue ocean with immaculate water, warm temperatures, and dewy-sweet air. Tahiti is also blessed with wide-open swell windows thanks to its situation in the South Pacific, and draws waves all year round.

On Tahiti Nui, the larger island of the two, barrier reef passes near Papeete, such as Matavai, will break best between November and February, when northerly swells drop down from the Aleutians. But the real deal around here occurs during the Tahitian wet season, as the closer, southern-hemisphere storm systems push surf onto the south and west coasts. During this period, waves from five feet (1.6 m) to fifteen feet (5 m) tall spark spots like Taapuna and Maraa to life, forming gaping, intense, expert-only, left-hand barrels.

Connected to the main island by a small isthmus, Tahiti Iti has two of French Polynesia's best-known lefts along its southwest shore: Vairao and Teahupoo. While Vairao is a classic, grinding, perfect tube, it is nowadays overshadowed by Teahupoo, one of the scariest and deadliest big waves on the planet.

Surf Tahiti

Location:
Pacific Ocean
Country:
Tahiti, part of French Polynesia
Language:
French and Tahitian, and some English
Currency:
CFP (Cour de Franc Pacifique)

The Good . . .
- Pristine surf
- Tropical scenery

And the Bad . . .
- Shallow coral reef
- Mosquitoes
- Expensive accommodations

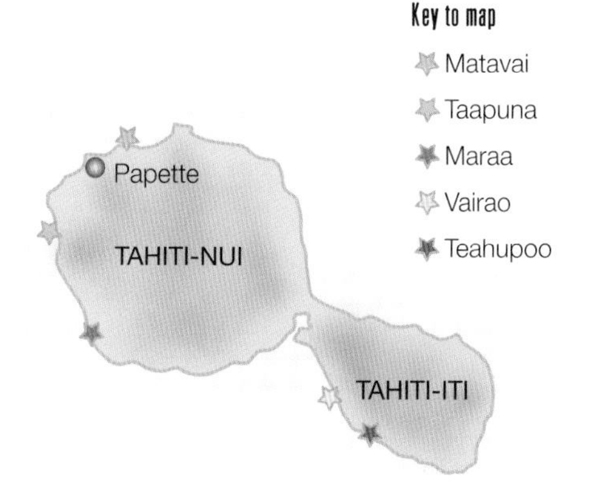

Key to map
- Matavai
- Taapuna
- Maraa
- Vairao
- Teahupoo

Below An aerial perspective of the unforgiving reef corner at Teahupoo and beyond.

"Big-wave riding is like an inner desire you have to challenge the sea or be in harmony with the sea in its most dynamic moment."

—Laird Hamilton from *Step into Liquid*

Teahupoo changes everything

The South Pacific Ocean region is rife with giant swells seeking a shallow reef to smash into. While several of Oceania's big waves, such as Shipstern Bluff and Cyclops, are worthy of discussion, everything is overshadowed by the Tahitian wave called Teahupoo.

When Teahupoo was first popularized in the 1990s, it rewrote the definition of a big wave. Reportedly first ridden in 1985 by Tahitian Thierry Vernaudon, followed by body boarders Mike Stewart and Ben Severson a few years later, Teahupoo swept into the collective surfing psyche. Though the sub-sea-level spot is not the tallest wave in the world, it is definitely the gnarliest. Any wipeout here, even when Teahupoo breaks small, can mean death. Formed by an ancient, freshwater river that flowed down from the mountains and eroded a path through the coral shelf, Teahupoo, which translates to "the end of the road," boasts the thickest lip, shallowest reef, and widest tubes anywhere. On big swells it would be easy to fit a city bus inside Teahupoo's titanic barrels.

Riding on the Shoulders of Giants

BILLABONG XXL GLOBAL
BIG WAVE AWARDS

Biggest Wave Award

2000–01 Mike Parsons, Cortes Banks
2001–02 Carlos Burle, Mavericks
2002–03 Makua Rothman, Jaws
2003–04 Pete Cabrinha, Jaws
2004–05 Dan Moore, Jaws
2005–06 Brad Gerlach, Todos Santos
2006–07 Greg Long, Dungeons
2007–08 Mike Parsons, Cortes Banks
2008–09 Grant Baker, Tafelberg Reef

Monster Paddle Award

2001–02 Paul Paterson, Waimea Bay
2002–03 Toby Cunningham, Todos Santos
2003–04 Zach Wormhoudt, Mavericks
2004–05 Shane Desmond, Mavericks
2005–06 Diego Medina, Punta de Lobos
2006–07 Garrett McNamara, Mavericks
2007–08 Greg Long, Todos Santos
2008–09 Derek Dunfee, Mavericks

Monster Tube Award

2003–04 Malik Joyeux, Teahupoo
2004–05 Dylan Longbottom, Shipstern Bluff
2005–06 Shane Dorian, Teahupoo
2006–07 Ken Collins, Puerto Escondido
2007–08 Manoa Drollet, Teahupoo
2008–09 Mark Healey, Yeti

Ride of the Year Award

2006–07 Ken Collins, Puerto Escondido
2007–08 Shane Dorian, Teahupoo
2008–09 Greg Long, Dungeons

Left Maui's Ian Walsh navigates the mutant chaos of Teahupoo on a monster swell.

Forecasting waves

Correctly predicting the arrival time, size, and duration of waves has been an ongoing struggle for surfers throughout much of the modern era. Forecasting swells once involved little more than blind guesswork and crossed fingers. Nowadays, it is as simple as turning on the computer.

Over the past sixty-plus years, the science of marine meteorology has improved exponentially. Once, crude isobar pressure charts and extensive mathematical equations were necessary to forecast incoming surf, and the results were sporadic at best. One of the earliest uses of wave forecasting occurred in World War II, when Allied forces enlisted oceanographers to develop a better way to predict oceanic conditions. The more-accurate information would be used to help them plan and execute beach landings, including the infamous D-Day amphibious assault at Normandy.

While these early wave models worked to some degree, the physics of how waves are created and move through the ocean was still unclear, and the accuracy of later versions depended on a better understanding of the scientific phenomenon. In the 1950s, the Miles-Phillips Theory was proposed, which clearly described how waves are really generated from a flat sea; this became the basis for all serious models that followed.

Soon, the information necessary to predict conditions was out there, but few surfers really knew how to get their hands on, let alone understand, marine forecasting charts and graphs. The big breakthrough for surfers came in 1985, when the Wave Model Development and Implementation group instituted a wave model to compute all the terms and equations necessary to calculate accurately, among other things, where, when, and how long wave activity would hit a particular region of coastline. Not coincidentally, upstart surf forecasting services began appearing after WAM, the Wave Analysis Model, was created.

Phone-message and fax surf reports filled the information gap for a short time, but they have since been replaced by the Internet. Instantaneously, the general surfing public gained access to a vast array of marine meteorological and surf-specific websites that present the information as easy-to-digest, animated wave models; color-coded forecasts; and weather buoy readings. You can even find live camera links to nearly every wave-pounded country in the world, making it easy to check the surf conditions at the mere click of a mouse.

Below Forecasting waves remains an inexact science; sometimes being wrong is cause for celebration.

More great surf areas

Producing a picturesque showcase of the fifty greatest surf destinations found on this watery planet proved a difficult task. So, in an effort to include a batch of those that came close to making the top fifty, here is a quick hit list of twenty-five more great surf areas to explore.

North America

Central California

An incredibly diverse region that stretches from Point Conception up to Santa Cruz, Central California is a beautiful run with a wide variety of wave types awaiting hardy surfers. Just be sure to respect the locals.

Florida

With waves on both its Atlantic and Gulf coasts, Florida's numerous beach breaks, jetties, and piers provide plenty of options to find playful surf, which gets a lot more serious when hurricane swells march in.

New Jersey

New Jersey, much like the rest of America's East Coast, is surrounded by sandy beach breaks that can get downright perfect when the right swells, sandbars, and weather conditions converge.

Nova Scotia

Part of the Maritime Provinces of Canada, Nova Scotia's burly shore holds a bevy of point breaks, reefs, and beach breaks for those willing to don serious rubber to combat the chilly water temps.

Central America

Nicaragua

Nicaragua's southern half of its western shoreline is loaded with impressive lefthanders. The country is blessed with warm water year-round and has constant offshore winds.

Dominican Republic

Dominican Republic, on the island of Hispaniola, receives swells from the Atlantic Ocean and the Caribbean Sea. Some of the nation's best reefs and beach breaks are found on its northern coast, called the Amber Coast.

Tortola

The largest of the British Virgin Islands and the capital of the region, the north shore of Tortola is home to world-class breaks like cane Garden Bay and Capoon's Bay. Beware of the psychedelic properties of the local mushroom tea.

South America

Fernando de Noronha

A tiny, volcanic island off the northeastern coast of Brazil, Fernando de Noronha's lack of a continental shelf allows powerful swells to arrive unfettered, producing punchy, hollow surf along its beaches and reefs.

Southern Brazil

The southern half of Brazil, north and south of Rio de Janeiro, offers an abundance of beach breaks, reefs, and even a few stellar rivermouth sandbars for those interested in more than the country's world-famous nightlife and carnival.

Europe

Norway

Norway's near-freezing ocean temperatures kept it out of the surfing spotlight for decades, but several surf-rich areas, such as the Lofoten archipelago, are now being exposed thanks to long point breaks and unmatched Arctic backdrops.

Northern Spain

Spain's northern coastal beaches hold far more than just the epic lefthanders at Mundaka. The beautiful region turns most North Atlantic swells into wondrous surf along its beaches and reefs.

Northwest France

While much of the national surfing focus is directed toward the country's southwestern shores, the northwest coast of France, encompassing Brittany, is less crowded and is full of quality reefs, point breaks, and gorgeous sandy beaches.

Fuerteventura (Canaries)
Fuerteventura, the second largest of the Canary Islands, has a wealth of surf potential, boasting more than 150 beaches, powerful lava reef breaks, and an unusual, desertlike environment.

Africa

Ghana
The tiny African country of Ghana may not get much surf media attention, but its fun right point breaks and warm water, combined with the dearth of local surfers, can make for an unforgettable, off-the-beaten-path surf vacation.

Mozambique
Mozambique's more than 1,500 miles (2,400 km) of coastline is wide open for surf exploration. Crowded lineups are rare, and scoring at top-shelf breaks like Tofinho and Ponta D'Ouro, is worth the effort alone.

Madagascar
The Earth's fourth-largest island is blessed with a natural ecosystem unlike any other on the planet. Plus Madagascar receives swells from three different directions. The island's offshore coral reefs and passes can be dangerous, but when the tide is right, they serve up magnificent waves.

Seychelles
Lying off the east coast of Africa, the clean, manageable surf around the Seychelles, especially on islands like Mahe, has lured surfers seeking exotic locales and mellow waves since the 1960s.

Asia

Philippines
The northern and eastern fringes of the Philippines are pristine regions full of beach breaks, fantastic reefs like Cloud 9 and Majestics, and, for those with a reliable global positioning system (GPS) and boat access, numerous undiscovered surf spots.

Andaman Islands
Governed by India and home to a number of native tribes, the Andaman Islands form an unspoiled archipelago that harbors a few of the world's best, and yet least publicized, reef waves.

Sumbawa
Sumbawa's south and west sides are stacked with classic, fast, and hollow, reef breaks like Yo-Yos, Super Suck, and Scar Reef. These beaches can offer respite from the heavy crowds and hustle-and-bustle of nearby Bali.

West Timor
West Timor's offshore islands, like Rote, Savu, and Dana, make the best of a limited swell window to create quick, barreling, down-the-line waves at some of Indonesia's least crowded lineups.

Oceania

Samoa
American and Western Samoa are raw, tropical surfing destinations with expansive swell windows, powerful volcanic and barrier reef waves, and an intriguing and friendly mix of cultures ashore.

Tonga
The four major island groups that make up the Tonga chain may be much less popular than its neighbor to the east, Fiji, but the reef break surf here can be equally as inviting with exponentially fewer surfers.

New Caledonia
The south-facing barrier-reef waves of New Caledonia require you to enlist boat charters or yachts in order to access them, but once at sea the area can become a surfer's personal paradise.

Tasmania
Tasmania, Australia's sixth state, has recently skyrocketed into the collective surf psyche thanks to frightening images of beastly rights at Shipstern Bluff. Thankfully, the rest of the island holds breaks that are much more forgiving and run the gamut of wave types.

Glossary of surfer terms

Aerial – *n.* any surfing maneuver where a surfer and his/her surfboard launches above the lip of a wave.

Air drop – *n.* a sketchy maneuver where a surfer and his/her board are momentarily lifted off the surface of a cresting or concave wave many times during the initial takeoff.

Barrel – *n.* see **Tube**

Beach break – *n.* a sandy bottom surf break, generally characterized by shifting sandbars and banks that create short rides and sometimes hollow conditions.

Double overhead – *adj.* term used to describe a wave that is twice as tall as the height of an average surfer.

Down the line (also **down-the-line**) – *n.* 1) the quick, walling section of a wave toward which surfer is projecting his/her ride.
– *adj.* 2) used to describe evenly tapered, streamline waves.

Foil – *n.* viewed lengthwise, the distribution of a surfboard's thickness from its nose to tail.

Free-surfer – *n.* a professional surfer who is paid by sponsors to surf but does not compete on the professional tours.

Goofyfoot (also **goofyfooter**) – *n.* a surfer who rides with his/her left foot back (on the tail) and right foot forward (at the front of the board).

Gremmie (also **gremmy** or **grommet**) – *n.* a young, usually pre-teen surfer.

Gun – *n.* blanket term used to describe a long, narrow, thin surfboard, usually constructed with a pintail, designed to handle large surf.

Haole – *n.* Hawaiian term literally translated to "without breath," but generally used to describe a white visitor, or anyone foreign to Hawaii.

Holding – *adj.* in possession of; slang term borrowed from drug dealing.

Laying it on rail (also **rail turning**) – *v.* completing a powerful, high-speed turn where the surfer buries the surfboard's inside rail, or outer edge, into wave face.

Left (or **lefthander**) – *n.* a wave that breaks from left to right when viewed from shore.

Longboarder – *n.* a surfer who mostly rides longboards.

North (also **north swell**) – *n.* a type of swell that moves from north to south.

Overhead – *adj.* term used to describe a wave that is taller than the height of an average surfer.

Paddle-in surfing – *n.* the conventional style of surfing, where a surfer lays prostrate on a surfboard and pulls himself/herself into a wave using only physical strength.

Peaky – *adj.* triangle-shaped or wedge-like, usually breaking both ways; a "peaky" wave is characterized by an A-frame look which creates both right and left shoulders.

Pintail – *n.* a surfboard design where the back of the board, or tail, is narrow and comes to a fine point, generally used to generate speed and paddle into big and/or demanding waves.

Point break – *n.* a surf break where waves wrap around a point of land that generally creates long, peeling waves.

Regular-footer (also **natural-footer**) – *n.* a surfer who rides with his/her right foot back (on the tail) and left foot forward.

Right (also **righthander**)–n. a wave that breaks from right to left when viewed from shore.

Roaring Forties – *n.* an impressive wave-generating region of the Indian Ocean on or near the 40-degree latitude line, found between the southern tip of Africa and southwestern edge of Australia.

Salty dog – *n.* an older, experienced, and sometimes bitter, surfer.

Shortboarder – *n.* a surfer who mostly rides shortboards.

Shoulder – *n.* the sloping section of wave ahead of the curl or peak that has not crested or become a wall.

Slab – *n.* a hollow, often thick and gnarly wave created when an ocean swell meets an extremely shallow segment of reef.

Snake – *v.* to drop in on a wave in front of another surfer who is already standing up and riding closer to the curl or peak; to cut off.

South (also **south swell**) – *n.* a type of swell that moves from south to north.

Swell window – *n.* the direction from which swells can reach a specific shore, unobstructed by islands, peninsulas or promontories and surrounding coastline; measured by angle degrees.

Tow-in surfing – n. a style of surfing invented in the late 1980s ad early '90s where the surfer is towed behind a small motorized watercraft, using a water-ski rope, and is swung into a wave before it crests.

Tube – *n.* the cylindrical, hollow interior of a wave, reaching from its crest to trough, created when the lip throws out in an arclike manner.

Wettie – *n.* an Australian slang term for wetsuit.

Bibliography

Books and periodicals

Ambrose, Greg. *Surfer's Guide to Hawaii: Hawaii Gets all the Breaks* (Honolulu: Bess Press, 1992)

Brown, DeSoto. *Surfing: Historic Images from the Bishop Museum Archives* (Honolulu: Bishop Museum Press, 2006)

Cralle, Trevor. *The Surfin'ary: A Dictionary of Surfing Terms and Surfspeak* (Berkeley: Ten Speed Press, 1991)

Currie, Stephen. *Australia and the Pacific Islands* (Farmington Hills: Thomson Gale, 2005)

Elwell, John C., Schmuass, Jane and the California Surf Museum. *Surfing in San Diego* (Chicago: Arcadia Press, 2007)

Finney, Ben and James D. Houston. *Surfing: A History of the Ancient Hawaiian Sport* (San Francisco: Pomegranate Artbooks, 1996)

Gault-Williams, Malcolm. *Legendary Surfers, Volume 1, 2500 B.C To 1910 A.D.* (USA: Malcolm Gault-Williams, 2005)

Green, Jonathan. *Cassell's Dictionary of Slang* (London: Cassell & Co, 2000)

Hall, Sandra Kimberly. *Duke: A Great Hawaiian* (Honolulu: Bess Press, 2004)

Kampion, Drew. *Stoked: A History of Surf Culture* (Layton: Gibbs Smith, 2003)

Marcus, Ben. *Surfing USA! An Illustrated History of the Coolest Sport of All Time* (Stillwater: Voyageur Press, 2005)

Nelson, Chris and Demi Taylor. *Surfing the World* (Bath, UK: Footprint Handbooks Ltd., 2006)

Sumpter, Rod. *100 Best Surf Spots in the World* (Guilford: The Globe Pequot Press, 2004)

Sutherland, Bruce. *The Stormrider Guide: Europe* (Bude, UK: Low Pressure Ltd., 2000)

–*The Stormrider Guide: North America* (Bude, UK: Low Pressure Ltd., 2002)

–*The World Stormrider Guide* (Bude (UK): Low Pressure Ltd., 2001)

–*The World Stormrider Guide*, Volume 2 (Bude, UK: Low Pressure Ltd., 2004)

Warshaw, Matt. *The Encyclopedia of Surfing* (USA: Harcourt, Inc., 2005)

Movies

Brown, Bruce. *The Endless Summer* (Torrance: Bruce Brown Films, 1966)

Peralta, Stacy. *Riding Giants* (Los Angeles: Agi Orsi Productions, 2004)

Campbell, Thomas. *The Seedling* (USA: Woodshed Productions, 1999)

Johnson, Jack and Chris Malloy. *Shelter* (USA: Woodshed Films, 2001)

Campbell, Thomas. *Sprout* (USA: Woodshed Films, 2008)

Internet Sources

Billabong XXL. http://www.billabongxxl.com

The Coastal Data Information Program. University of California, San Diego, http://cdip.ucsd.edu

Mavericks: The Wave Beyond. http://maverickssurf.com

National Oceanic and Atmospheric Administration. United States Department of Commerce, http://www.noaa.gov

Surf Art.com. Waterman Surf Art Gallery, http://www.surfart.com

Surfing for Life: A Film. http://surfingforlife.com

Surfline: Know Before You Go. Surfline/Wavetrack Inc., http://www.surfline.com

Wannasurf!. Wannasurf.com Ltd., http://wannasurf.com

WaveWatch: Waves, Weather, News. Source Interlink Media, http://www.wavewatch.com

WetSand. http://wetsand.com

Picture Credits / Acknowledgments

Cover

Sean Davey/Australian Picture Library/Corbis: FC central image
Scott Aichner/A-Frame: FC & BC background image

Inside pages

A-Frame: **A-Frame/Aichner,** 2–3 background image; **/Anders,** 152–153; **/Carey,** 67; **/DeCamp,** 46; **/Divine,** 57; **/Grambeau,** 170–171; **/J. Kimball,** 80–81; **/Kottke,** 77, 167; **/Marti,** 49; **/Merkel,** 150–151; **/Mez,** 51, 109; **/Miller,** 73; **/Reposar,** 52–53; **/Stacy,** 45
Aquashot/poullenot: 76, 92, 98, 99
Don Balch: 17, 43, 68bl, 68–69bm
Courtesy of Boardwalk Surf Ltd: 5, 38 second from left, 38 far right, 39 middle, 39 second from right
Jamie Bott: 61, 104
Courtesy of California Surf Museum Archive: 11, 14, 20l, 20r, 107tl, 107bl, 145tm, 145bm
J.S. Callahan/tropicalpix: 44, 58, 59, 66, 68t, 91, 105, 108, 133, 166
Matthew Clark: 48
Mike Conroy: 128m, 129tl, 129bl
Corbis: **Corbis/Bettmann,** 10, 12, 15; **/Ashley Cooper,** 102; **/Fridmar Damm,** 110; **/Sean Davey/Australian Picture Library,** 1, 3; **/Rick Doyle,** 37; **/Fadil,** 135; **/Philippe Giraud/Sygma,** 90; **/Dave G. Houser,** 132; **/Hulton-Deutsch Collection,** 8–9; **/Ken Kaminesky/Take 2 Productions,** 145l; **/Lake County Museum,** 140; **/Roy Morsch,** 144t; **/Michael Ochs Archives,** 144br; **/Doug Pearson/JAI,** 155; **/David Pu'u,** 4–5/38–39/175; **/Bob Winsett,** 72
Ryan Craig: 29, 30, 31, 62
Sean Davey: 19t, 53, 100, 124–125, 126, 127, 141, 142–143, 146, 147, 148, 149, 157, 158–159, 160, 162–163, 163, 169
Steve Fitzpatrick: 64, 65, 114, 115
geoffreyragatz.com: 60, 74, 75, 78–79, 81, 168
Alan van Gysen: 6–7, 47, 69br, 84–85 (repeated on inside front cover), 89, 94–95, 95, 120, 130, 131, 134
Devon Howard: 19b, 41, 122–123, 165
iStockphoto: **/aurumarcus,** 68br (graphic); **/Marina Strizhak,** 144 (background); **/P_Wei,** 34
JohnLymanPhotos: 21m, 21b
Pedro Duarte Jorge: 113
Tom Keck: 16
The Kobal Collection: 107r; **Kobal/Bruce Brown Films,** 106; **/Columbia,** 107ml
John Lamb: 128–129
Courtesy of Library of Congress: 13 (LC-B2-2427-11)
maggiemarsek.com: 38 far left, 38 middle, 38 second from right, 39 far left, 39 second from left, 39 far right
Sonny Miller/World Wave Pictures: 18, 69t, 171
Moonwalker: 26, 27, 28–29, 156, 161, 164
NARC: 33
Brian Nevins: 86, 87
Nunn: 101
Bob Penuelas: 129tr
David Pu'u: 32, 35, 121
Schutz: 138, 139
Shutterstock: **Shutterstock/Alan Freed,** 42; **/Jennifer Johnson, BlueCherry Graphics,** 145r; **/Graham S. Klotz,** 50; **/musicman,** 144bl; **/Andre Nantel,** 56; **/Carlos Sanchez Pereyra,** 40; **/Luis M. Seco,** 63; **/Rui Vale de Sousa,** 112; **/Stefanie van der Vinden,** 93; **/Vatikaki,** 88
Lance Smith: 36
Mickey Smith: 103, 111, 116–117, 154
Steele: 143
Courtesy of Surf World Archive: 21t
Terrametrics (satellite images), 29, 36, 42, 48, 62, 74, 98, 108, 112, 115, 125, 132, 158, 166

Ryan A. Smith would like to thank Marisa Breyer, Jane Schmauss, Tom Glenn, John Lamb, Barry Haun, John Lyman, Drew Kampion, Don Balch, Devon Howard, Jeff Hall, Bowen Ota, Bill Parr, Lance Smith, Moonwalker, Al Ashworth, Jon Steele, Sean Davey, Michael Kew, David Pu'u, Alan van Gysen, Geoff Ragatz, Steve Fitzpatrick, Tara Torburn, Sonny Miller, Darin Daly, David Alton Dickey, Jamie Bott, CSM, ISM, SHF, Surf World, Bishop Museum, Betty Kam, Ric Riavac, Desoto Brown, Paulo Espinoza, Emily Vizoo, Julie Cox, Todd Quinn, Isaac Brock, Tom Keck, Julius Zolezzi, Ben Marcus, Patrick Giles, John Austin, Glen Dubock, Bob Penuelas, Grant Ellis, Howard @ Drift, Tim Nunn, Mickey Smith, Bobby Schutz, John S. Callahan, Matthew Clark, Ryan Craig, David Franzen, Jim Kempton, Bill Sharp, Billabong XXL, Red Bull BWA, Brain Nevins, Marcus Sanders, Art Brewer, Joao Valente, Larent Masurel, Pedro Duarte Jorge, Chris Christenson, Rich Pavel, Scott Hulet, Jeff Divine, Damien Poullenot, J.P. St. Pierre, Maggie Marsek, Boardwalk Surf Ltd., Bonnie Szumski, *Slide* Magazine, and everyone else who had a hand in helping me make this book possible.

Editors' acknowledgments: Thanks to Terrametrics (www.terrametrics.com) for permission to screen-grab selected satellite images; to Boardwalk Surf Ltd, Newquay, UK, for permission to reproduce selected surfboard images; to Mike Conroy, for front covers from his comic collection. Thanks also to Bonnie Vandewater at Thunder Bay Press, for her careful attention to detail during the production of this book.